COMPLETE**TECHNIQUE**
FORMODERN**GUITAR**

Third Edition

JOSEPH**ALEXANDER**

FUNDAMENTAL**CHANGES**

Complete Technique for Modern Guitar

Third Edition

Published by **www.fundamental-changes.com**

ISBN: 978-1-78933-074-8

Copyright © 2018 Joseph Alexander

The moral right of this author has been asserted.

www.fundamental-changes.com

Twitter: **@guitar_joseph**

Over 10,000 fans on Facebook: **FundamentalChangesInGuitar**

Instagram: **FundamentalChanges**

For over 250 Free Guitar Lessons with Videos Check Out

www.fundamental-changes.com

Contents

Expressive Techniques 73

Introduction

There is a common idea among many guitarists that excellent instrumental technique is something that takes years to master. They believe that technique should be put before all else and that it should occupy the majority of your practice time.

In my experience this is not the case, and actually, an over-enthusiastic, single-minded pursuit of 'perfect' technique can be counterproductive, unnecessary, and even damaging to your health.

There is a simple question that you should be asking yourself with regards to technique. It's a question that is obvious but is missed by the majority of guitarists that I teach. When I was first asked this question by my guitar teacher back at the Guitar Institute in London, it floored me, as my teacher had the best technique I'd ever seen.

Now, when I ask my own students the same question fifteen years later, they give me the exact same reaction. The question is:

'How much technique do you need?'

Think about the question, what does it mean to you?

We all pick up the guitar for different reasons. I saw a video of Hendrix at Monterey when I was four years old. That was closely followed by Queen at Live Aid in '85, and then I was hooked. Now I have over forty private guitar students, and on the first lesson I ask each one why they want to play the guitar. I think it's important to keep this original goal in mind when we get drawn into an endless spiral of technique practice.

Many students say they want to play music for their friends, some want to write their own stuff, some want to play blues, country, progressive rock or 'screamo' metal.

Some guys are simply honest and say that they want to impress girls!

Whatever the goal is (and if you don't have one, get one), you should certainly consider that the majority of musical styles didn't evolve as a result of technical excellence (with some notable exceptions).

If you want to play blues, for example, you need solid technique. You do not need to spend 8 hours a day practicing *only* technique; you need to play some blues. If you want to play Dream Theater, you clearly need to spend a lot more time working on technique, but you can't *only* practice technique, you actually need to learn some Dream Theater songs too.

Learning to play songs is where you discover what technique exercises you need to practice! Simply find out where you get stuck in the song and work out what it is you can't do. Don't make the mistake of thinking that you should have everything in place before you attempt the song.

One of the best players on the planet said, 'I never practiced technique, I just played songs and tried to figure out what it was that I couldn't do, and why I couldn't do it.'

Hopefully that is some food for thought.

All that aside (and because I'm certainly not suggesting you *don't* buy this book!), there is still the misconception that developing good technique takes years of focused and dedicated practice.

That is where this book comes in.

I have been teaching guitar as my full-time job for over eighteen years, and I've been lucky enough to study under some of the best guitarists in the country. During my career, I have whittled down the list of exercises that I give to my students, to only the ones that give massive benefits, extremely quickly.

As you can probably tell, I'm not a massive 'giver of exercises', but I do see the same fundamental technical problems crop up time and time again. In fact, most of my students will have used most of the exercises in this book to solve most of their technical challenges on the guitar.

These are the exercises that really work. They will address the problems you are having right now, and are probably the reason you're reading this book. If an exercise doesn't look like it will challenge you or teach you something, please skip it. There is never any reason to practice something you can already do.

This book is split into four sections,

- Picking & Finger Independence
- Rhythm
- Legato
- Expressive Techniques

You will sometimes see similar exercises in different sections of the book, albeit with a different focus. There are some finger independence exercises which, for example, make great legato studies due to the finger combinations used. Don't be put off by this; there is no point reinventing the wheel each time we work on a new area of technique. Indeed, when you have studied similar exercises from a new perspective, you will often find a new weakness to work on.

For 90% of you, rhythm and picking should certainly be your first priority. I fully appreciate you may have other challenges, so feel free to dive in where you want.

Remember this though: Your rhythm isn't as good as you think it is. Unless you're Mike Stern, you would benefit from taking a look at the rhythm section first. About 60% of my own practice these days is rhythm. That should tell you something.

I would go as far as to say that the whole point of learning technique, in my eyes, is *rhythm* and *freedom of expression*. Most professional guitarists I have spoken to agree entirely, although most would put *'freedom of expression'* first.

Speed:
Good technique does not mean playing fast, and playing fast does not mean good technique. There are however certain 'industry standard' tempos you should have in the back of your mind as goals.

Picking:
1/16th notes should be clean at 120bpm. Some would argue 140bpm, and if you're into shred metal, you'll probably want to hit 160bpm.

1/16th-note triplets should be at least 100bpm.

Legato:
The sky's the limit, so long as *every* note is defined and even across the beat.

Every example in this book is demonstrated as an audio file. You can download the audio examples from **www.fundamental-changes.com/audio-downloads**

Don't forget that it's normally much more useful to be able to execute any exercise *extremely* slowly and accurately, than to play it at lightning speed.

Pain:

If you have **any** pain, stop *immediately* and see a specialist. If your posture is good and your technique is good you should never experience any pain. The most common reason is that you're trying to play too fast too soon, but you should still stop and see a specialist.

Finally, remember our original goal of musicality. Keep in mind *you are what you practice*. If you only practice technical exercises, then that is all you will ever play. Learn music.

Joseph Alexander

Get The Audio

The audio files for this book are available to download for *free* from **www.fundamental-changes.com** and the link is in the top right corner. Simply select this book title from the drop-down menu and follow the instructions to get the audio.

We recommend that you download the files directly to your computer, not to your tablet and extract them there before adding them to your media library. You can then put them on your tablet, iPod or burn them to CD. On the download page there is a help PDF and *we also provide technical support through the form on the download page.*

We spend a long time getting the audio just right and you will benefit greatly from listening to these examples as you work through the book. They're free, so what are you waiting for?!

Head over to **www.fundamental-changes.com** and grab the audio files now.

There are also over 250 free guitar lessons to get your teeth into.

If you're reading this book on an eReader, double-tap each image to enlarge it. It can help to hold your eReader in landscape mode and turn off column viewing.

Picking and Finger Independence

While clearly not the same thing, it is difficult to give useful finger independence exercises which don't involve some degree of pick control.

It's a tricky 'chicken or egg' situation, but we have to start somewhere. As many apparent 'picking' problems are caused by a hidden fretting hand weakness, we will start with finger independence in the fretting hand.

The most common problems I see regarding finger independence involve a lack of dexterity between the 2nd and 3rd fingers, and weakness in the 4th finger.

Lack of dexterity between the 2nd and 3rd fingers:

Each finger in your hand has its own tendon, except for the 2nd and 3rd fingers, which share one. Due to this human, physical idiosyncrasy, our 2nd and 3rd fingers do not like to work independently. Lay your fretting hand gently down on a desk and try to repeatedly switch between raising just the 3rd, and then just the 2nd finger. Compare that with lifting your 1st and 2nd finger…. You will see that a large part of building finger independence is learning to control these wayward fingers.

Weakness in the 4th finger:

Generally, the modern method of playing is to use the 3rd finger as much as possible, especially in those pentatonic bends. While I'm all for this, it can lead to a weakness in the 4th finger due to it not getting enough exercise. Strength and accuracy in the pinkie can often be the limiting factor in building speed and fluency.

The following exercises specifically target the previous two areas for concern.

Finger Independence Exercises

Permutations

This exercise was given to me by Shaun Baxter, an incredible player and educator who taught me while I studied at the Guitar Institute in London. Essentially, the idea is to target the weaknesses between any possible finger combinations on the fretboard. The key to building strength and control, at least for examples 1a and 1b, is to *hold your first finger down throughout.*

Example 1a:

Before you play this exercise, study the notes in brackets. The notes on the 6th and 7th frets move backwards and forwards across three strings while the notes on the 5th and 8th frets stay constant on the 4th string.

Hold down your 1st finger throughout and play the example, repeating it four times. This is tricky at first and will cause your hands to get fatigued quickly, so don't play it for longer than thirty-second bursts.

At all times, these examples are to be played one finger per fret. You should not use the same finger twice. Use your 1st finger on the 5th fret, 2nd on the 6th etc.

After thirty seconds of playing the example, take a break of fifteen seconds and then study example 1b:

Example 1b:

As you can see, this is the same idea, however the bracketed notes are reversed. Play through the whole idea as you did in example 1a. Keep playing for 30 seconds.

Next, swap the first two notes around:

Example 1c:

Finally, *keep* the first two notes swapped and swap the second two notes:

Example 1d:

We have now covered every fingering permutation in this sequence.

Practice the above four sequences slowly, set your metronome to 40 bpm and play two notes for each click. This example isn't about speed, and practicing it quickly will make it less beneficial.

The next sequence of notes to practice is this:

Example 2a:

It's the same idea, but the repeated notes are now in the middle. Here are the other three permutations of the above:

Example 2b:

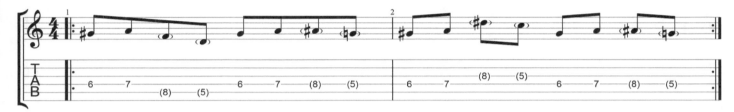

Example 2c:

Example 2d:

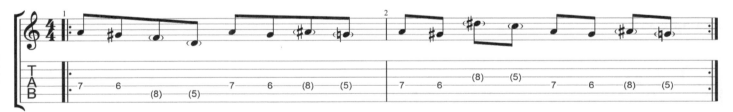

There are two other sets of possibilities to work on.

Example 3a:

Example 3b:

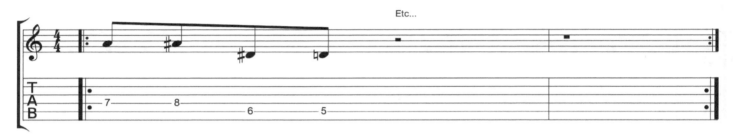

Example 3c:

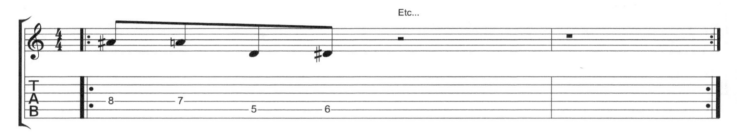

Example 3d:

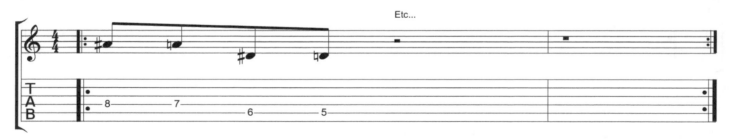

Now try this pattern:

Example 4a:

Example 4b:

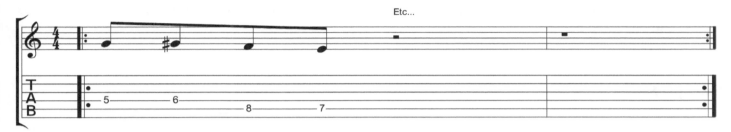

Example 4c:

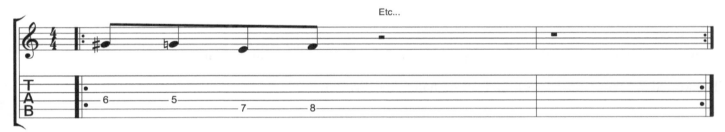

Example 4d:

For *all* of the preceding examples take the following approach:

1) Play for thirty seconds, take a fifteen second break, and then move to the next example.

2) Aim to play every example in a practice session. Playing through all examples in this way should take no more than ten minutes at the start of your practice routine.

3) If you find you can do an example comfortably, either play it slower or don't bother practicing it. There is no point practicing something you can already play.

4) When you can pick every note in each example, try using *hammer-ons* and *pull-offs*.

5) Playing this in a controlled, slow legato manner is a great example for control.

6) If the examples get too easy, try playing them with a slow swing feel, accenting every second note as demonstrated below.

Example 5a:

As with any kind of example, if you experience any type of pain, stop immediately.

The key to success is to control the fretting hand at a slow tempo.

4th Finger Strength

The following idea was given to me as a warm up example when I was about 13 years old. I've never been one to cling to old material, but this workout for your 3rd and 4th finger is golden. Whenever I have taken a break from guitar for a while, this is one of the first exercises I come back to.

Example 6a:

The example works by gradually placing the 3rd and 4th finger combination under increasing strain as you move across the fretboard.

Begin by slowly playing through example 6a, taking care to use the correct fingers on each fret as they're marked in the example. Once you have placed your 1st finger on the 5th fret, **keep it down** until you need to change strings.

As you move towards the bass string, the tendons in your wrist become gradually more stretched. Normally this causes the example to become progressively more difficult. Start by playing the 1/16th notes at 40bpm and make sure you can play across all strings evenly before speeding up. I'd be aiming for a maximum bpm of about 100. Faster is fine, but you must be able to play a constant tempo throughout the whole example.

When you can manage 40bpm evenly across all string, increase the metronome speed in increments of 8bpm.

The next example combines 4th finger strength with 2nd and 3rd finger independence:

Example 6b:

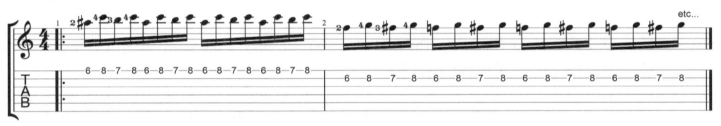

Example 6b is similar to example 6a, however will now hold down your 2nd finger on each string while working out your 3rd and 4th finger. This is much more challenging and beneficial, but once again, it is extremely important to go slowly and keep all the movements controlled.

Start by practicing this example without a metronome, before learning to control your fingers at 40bpm.

Picking

The examples in this section are some of the most useful ideas I've ever seen, and many of the ideas in the following chapters are derived from this useful, efficient system.

Alternate Picking V's Economy Picking

This is a debate that I am not going to wade into too deeply, however I should say that I am an economy picker.

If you're not clear of the difference, a simple explanation would be that an alternate picker picks up/down/up/down constantly, and often relies on the movement of the pick to execute rhythms accurately. An economy picker takes the most efficient direction between two points, but may have to work a little harder on playing an accurate rhythm.

This is an over-simplistic description, so before you start writing bad reviews and sending me hate mail I'm fully aware that this isn't the full story! The examples in this chapter are designed to teach economy picking because I've noticed much less injury and better time (generally) in players who use economy, rather than alternate picking.

If you want to alternate pick the following examples please go right ahead. You'll still learn a great deal.

A Description of Economy Picking

The main principle behind economy picking is that you should cross the strings with the plectrum as *little* as possible.

Play a down-pick on the open 5th string. The next note you will play is the open 4th string. In terms of efficiency, does it make sense to play the 4th string with a down-pick or an up-pick?

The answer is that you should always do another down-pick on the 4th string, because by doing an up-pick, you would have had to move across the 4th string without picking it before you were able to do the up pick. Why not just pick it on the way down to avoid the extra movement?!

A simple way to surmise would be:

• Every time you change strings away from your body, (down towards the floor), always use a down-pick

Of course, the opposite is true too:

• Every time you change strings towards your body (up towards the ceiling), always use an up-pick

• When playing a series of notes on the *same* string, alternate the pick direction.

These are the *only* three rules of economy picking. They cover every single possibility that can occur in your picking hand.

If you follow these rules while tackling the rest of this chapter you will start to notice your picking hand making smaller and smaller movements. There will be an increase in your accuracy, speed and fluency on the guitar, and a reduced chance of picking up injuries such as tendonitis or carpel tunnel syndrome.

In my opinion, the most amazing thing about economy picking is that once you have it sorted, you never have to worry about your picking again. You never waste your practice time wondering how to execute a particular rhythm.

Picking Hand Position

It is a difficult thing to explain in words, but the form of your picking hand is crucial. The heel, (the fleshy part of your hand that is in line with your little finger), should **always** be inlight contact with the bass strings, when you pick notes on the top strings. This not only allows you to easily locate the strings with your plectrum, it keeps down unwanted string noise when you play with distortion. If you can't reach the top strings in this position, **move your whole wrist lower on the guitar.**

Do *not* anchor your picking hand firmly to the guitar strings. If you want to play un-muted notes on the bass strings, move your wrist so that the heel rests gently on the guitar body.

If you were to ascend a scale over all six strings, your pick should be able to move in a straight line down the strings as you drop your whole wrist. If you anchor your wrist to the bass strings you will 'draw' an arc with the pick. This is to be avoided at all costs.

Tuck the fingers you are not using (2nd, 3rd and 4th) away, gently under your palm.
The plectrum should be held on the *side* of the 1st finger (not the pad) with the thumb gently supporting it on top. You should have about 2mm or 1/8" protruding from your thumb.

Picking Efficiency

Study **example 7a:**

Before worrying about how to correctly pick this example, make sure you can finger the notes using the '1 finger per fret' rule. Use your 1st finger for any 5th fret note, your 2nd finger for any 6th fret note, and so on.

Now, let us pay attention to the picking direction. This may be completely new for you so please go extremely slowly: Don't play a single note until you're *sure* you are going to be using the correct picking direction.

The point where you will most likely have a challenge is between **beat two-&**, and **beat three,** because here, there are two up-picks in a row. This, as hopefully you are aware is because you are changing from the 2nd to the 3rd string and we are avoiding an unnecessary crossing of the 3rd string.

When you have managed to play through this example correctly, set your metronome to 60 bpm and play the example as it is written above. Make sure you are focusing on picking direction, not the notes in your fretting hand. If you play a wrong note at this stage don't worry as long as the picking is correct.

If you're absolutely sure that your picking is correct, gradually increase the speed of your metronome by increments of 8bpm and work your way up to 100bpm.

Stop at 100bpm because we will be discussing how to increase speed properly later in the chapter.

Now, imagine the sequence of notes you have been playing is a cycle with no beginning or end. We can start playing at any point in that cycle and by doing this, we can not only focus on our picking, but also on any timing weaknesses in the fretting hand. This will become clear when you play through **example 7b:**

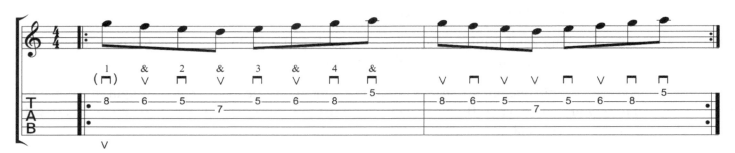

First, notice that the first down-pick is in brackets. You only play it as a down-pick on the first time through the cycle. On any repeat, it will be preceded by a note on the 1st string (beat four-and) so you must change strings with an up-pick.

Occasionally we get these little idiosyncrasies but they do not affect our approach to picking at all. Be *aware* that your picking is changing, but all you need to concentrate on is staying in rhythm.

As mentioned on the previous page, by starting this cycle of notes at different points, we can 'spotlight' any weaknesses in our picking technique, and make our practice time much more efficient.

Play through example 7b with your metronome set to 60bpm. Concentrate on first making sure your picking is correct before gradually raising the tempo by 8bpm each time you feel comfortable. There is no reason to hang around at one tempo if you can do it, so don't waste your practice time!

This first 'rotation' of the example will draw attention to any weaknesses you have when changing from the 1st finger on the 1st string to the 4th finger on the 2nd string. It's a common area for guitarists to struggle with, so as you gradually speed up the metronome, look out for the notes on beats four, 'four-and', and one becoming sloppy. The remainder of this example, combined with the 'How to Speed Up' section of this book will help a great deal with any weakness in your technique.

To continue this important example, we will start from every point in its cycle. Occasionally your picking direction will change slightly after the first loop, but stay focused on always using the correct direction as marked in the example.

Picking Rotations Continued

Example 7c:

Example 7d:

Example 7e:

Example 7f:

Example 7g:

Example 7h:

Initially, play through each example extremely slowly as it takes time to build new motor skills. Playing it correctly is much more important than playing it quickly. When you do gradually start to speed up, ensure you can play through each rotation at least eight times correctly before moving on to the next.

Once you have developed good directional control in your picking hand, and you are building speed and fluency, it pays to treat the previous series of examples as a set of rhythm tests.

Certain points of the cycle have a tendency to be rushed; the three notes on the 2nd string, for example, will tend to run into each other. Other areas will trip you up, like the previously mentioned change between string 1 and string 2. Be conscious of spacing each note *evenly* across the click. A great way to focus on this is to set your metronome to 40bpm and play 1/16th notes (four even notes per click).

Record yourself practicing, either on video or just audio and listen back to your playing regularly. You will soon see if you are rushing or falling behind the beat. This idea is covered in more depth in the *legato timing* chapter.

How to Speed Up

I once took on a student who was trying to develop his speed chops by increasing the metronome by 1 beat per minute each day, and playing everything he knew until after 'one hundred days', he'd have 'mastered the guitar'.

It's an interesting theory certainly, however in my experience this is not the quickest or most permanent way to build speed and control.

Speed is funny in that it's simply a case of developing a set of motor skills, and anyone, barring impairment, can develop phenomenal speed on the guitar. There will always be the YouTube videos of amazing twelve year old guitarists burning through scales to humble us into practicing just that bit harder.

If you look a little deeper however, often the actual rhythm of what the 'shredder' is playing can be a bit lax.[1]

The problem is that as the click gets faster, the distance between individual notes is reduced, and it becomes harder to know whether those blazing 1/16th-note triplets are entirely accurate. It *is* possible to tell, but generally the whole music (or example) comes across as a bit sloppy, or *floaty* against the pulse.

The answer lies simply in fretting hand control, and the majority of this work is carried out in the *legato timing* chapter later in the book. However, we should certainly take a look at the important concept of speed while studying picking.

The good news is that you do not have to practice *everything* you know as a speed example.

There are certain finger combinations and patterns in rock guitar that crop up time and time again, so these are the best place to start. Sometimes, when you're learning a new piece of music you may come across a unique challenge which requires work, but it's a waste of time to plan for that in advance. Work on it when you meet it.

Taking a previous example as our workhorse, let's focus again on **example 7a:**

Example 7a:

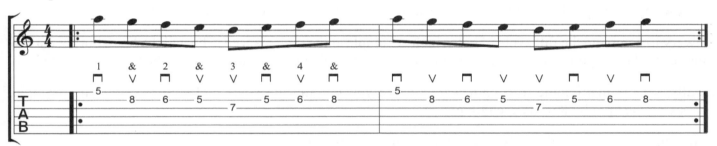

Make sure you can play this example cleanly and with the correct picking before attempting this example.

Set the metronome to 60 bpm and record yourself playing through the above example four times.

Listen to, or watch your recording. If the notes are evenly spaced across the beat, increase the metronome by 8bpm. It is important that you're honest with yourself here.

If you get to 100bpm, halve the metronome speed to 50, and **double up** the speed of your notes so you are now playing 1/16th notes:

---

1. This is by all means a generalisation and not always true. Many shredders have excellent time.

Example 7a played as 16th notes:

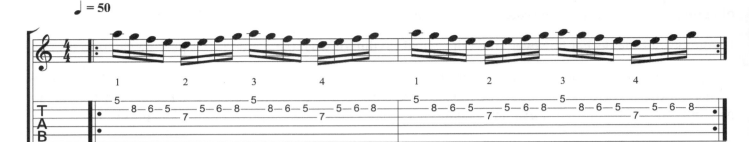

Repeat steps one and two until you find a point at which you're either struggling to play the example, or the rhythm starts to break down.

Reduce the metronome speed by 20% and *single out the specific part of the example you can't do*. This might be a couple of notes over a string change, or it could be the speed at which you are able to alternate pick the notes on the 2nd string. Whatever it happens to be, single it out and practice that part only.

Increase the metronome speed by *40bpm* and continue to play *only the part of the example that you're struggling with*. This should be nearly impossible, but try to do it a few times.

Don't worry about perfect timing initially, just try to target the clicks on the metronome.

Now try to complete the full cycle of notes in the example at the higher speed. This will be hard, but try it a few times even though you won't make it. Don't worry about perfect timing, just try to hit the first note on the beat.

Finally, set the metronome to 5 bpm *below* where you initially got stuck and continue with the example, increasing the bpm by 8 beats each time[2].

Using this precise method builds speed and technique extremely quickly.

The most important part of the process is when you raise the metronome speed to a point where you could never hope to complete the example. Working there, even for thirty seconds, makes your unconscious perceive the example at the lower tempo as much easier.

You don't need to record yourself *every* time you increase by 8bpm but it's a good idea to keep tabs on your rhythm by recording yourself regularly.

Of course, you need to practice this with every rotation of the example. Different rotations will have different challenges and technical difficulties. When you tackle the other rotations though, don't start with 1/8th notes. Begin with 1/16th notes at 50bpm to save yourself a lot of time. Obviously slow down if it's too fast to get started, but remember that you should only practice what you *can't* do.

See everything as a rhythm exercise. When you play 1/16th notes, every fifth note should be on the beat. If you're counting, you should be saying out loud:

1e&a 2e&a 3e&a 4e&a

---

2. If you're playing the exercise as 1/16th notes, you may want to increase the speed by just 4 or 5 bpm.

Make sure that your ones, twos, threes and fours fall *directly* on the beat.

It is important to tap your foot. It might sound simple, but by making the pulse a physical movement of your body, rather than a sound wave bouncing around the air, it will automatically make you play more in time. If you can't tap your foot accurately with this example, slow the beat right down and practice until you can.

Further Patterns

The previous examples should be altered to include different possible finger combinations. First apply the previous ideas to 8a-8h, to train your 3rd and 4th fingers. (Use your third on the B string, 7th fret).

Example 8a:

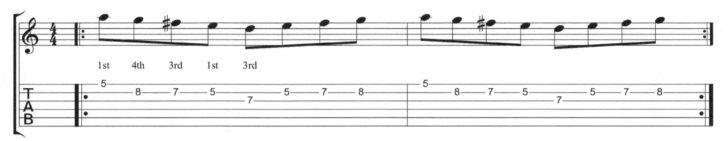

Example 8b:

Example 8c:

Example 8d:

Example 8e:

Example 8f:

Example 8g:

Example 8h:

Another essential (and common) finger combination is the one shown in examples 9a-9h.

Use the 4th, 2nd and 1st fingers to play the notes on the 2nd string. Continue to use the 3rd finger on the 3rd string.

Example 9a:

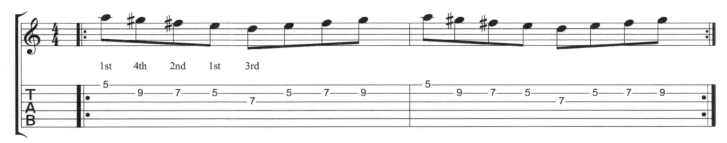

Example 9b:

Example 9c:

Example 9d:

Example 9e:

Example 9f:

Example 9g:

Example 9h:

String Skipping

When you economy pick over a string skip, (literally, missing out one string), the same picking rules apply.

Study the following example:

Example 10:

This is an idea based on a John Petrucci (Dream Theater) exercise where you 'spider' your way up the guitar neck. When you ascend the first four notes of each bar, use the fingering, 1, 2, 3, 4. Reverse that pattern for the last four notes. This example differs from the classic Petrucci exercise because here, the whole thing is economy picked.

Only the first four bars are shown, but continue the example up the neck until you reach the 12th fret. When you're there, descend the neck back down to the first fret as shown.

Example 10b:

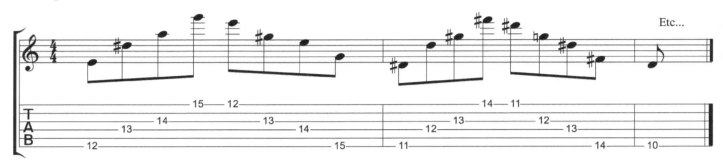

Throughout the example, your pick should look like its making a slow, broken strum across the strings. You only change direction after playing the 1st and 6th strings.

Useful Scale Examples

The following scalic ideas are included here as something of a 'dictionary' of modern melodic approaches. They are technically demanding in both hands and certainly great examples, but by studying them in the previously described manner, they will also train your ears to hear intervals, triads and arpeggios. As such, they are of massive help when breaking away from any tendency to 'run scales' while soloing.

Remember, you are what you practice: If you only practice repeated ascending and descending scales, that is all you will play when it is time to be creative. Creativity in practice leads to creativity in playing.

It would be easy here to give you a standard 'speed' three-note-per-string major scale. I have deliberately avoided doing so. By using a scale shape with a combination of two and three notes per string you will develop your technique much more rapidly. It will be slightly harder in the short term, but give you a much better all-round technique.

An important point to consider is that if something is *really* technically difficult, you should question whether there is any benefit to you to practice it. Normally there will be two or three places on the guitar where you can re-finger exactly the same notes much more easily. Why not simply do that? Also, if you spend hours working on something that is completely unnatural to play, you will end up 'locked' into playing that idea when you solo. You won't be able to play anything else!

With that in mind, consider how you're spending time. With only limited hours in a day to practice, it's vital to be selective about your technical studies.

All the following examples are based around the following scale shape of A Major:

Example 11:

Make sure you can play this perfectly. Start with the metronome at the fastest speed at which you can comfortable play the shape ascending and descending, and increase the metronome in 8bpm increments until you can play it smoothly in 1/16th notes at 120bpm.

An interval is the distance between two notes. For example, C – D is a 2nd. C – E is a 3rd. We will now study the scale of A Major in 3rds, ascending and descending.

Example 12a:

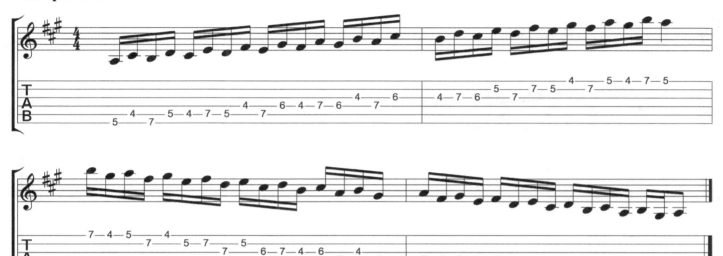

Your target for this example should be 1/16th notes at 100bpm, although there is no need to stop there.

Next, here is A Major in 4ths. Again, aim for 100bpm:

Example 12b:

A Major in 6ths[3]:

Example 12c:

Here are some useful scale patterns that are often used to build technique and melodic phrases. They should all be played to 120 bpm.

Example 13a:

Example 13b:

---

3. 5ths aren't commonly used.

Example 13c:

Example 13d:

There are many more possible patterns, so try inventing your own.

The next series of examples really start to break up the scale. They're *triads*. You can think of them as 'stacked 3rds'.

Example 14a:

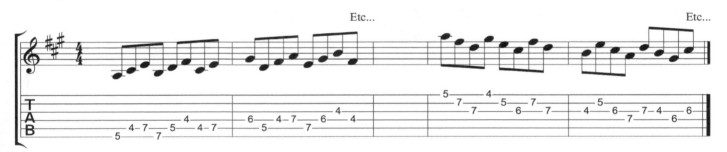

Example 14b:

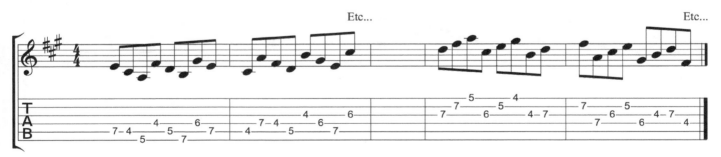

Example 14c:

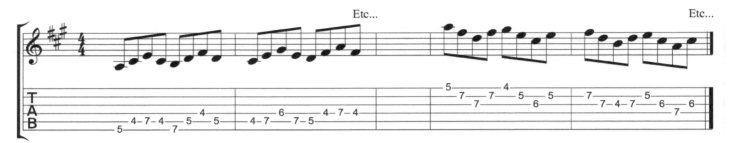

Example 14d:

Finally, here are ideas based on the four-note arpeggios formed from each scale step. These are much more technically demanding, so go slowly and always use the correct picking.

Example 15a:

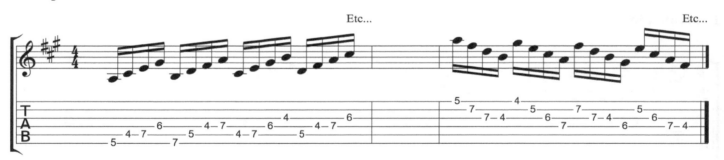

Example 15b:

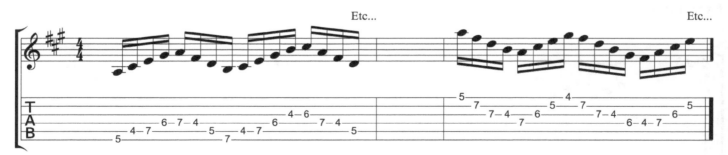

Example 15c:

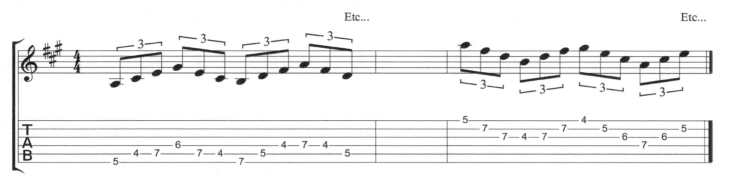

Again, there are many possible permutations when it comes to arpeggio patterns like this. Try to invent your own.

1/16th-Note Triplets

An important part of modern rock guitar playing revolves around lines of aggressive 1/16th-note triplets. Personally, I'm more comfortable playing these in a legato style, however the 'shrapnel' 1/16th-note triplets of players like Paul Gilbert and Nuno Bettencourt are an important rhythm to have at your disposal.

Again, the main obstacle to playing these triplets well is rhythm. Picking is certainly an easier approach rhythmically, but can limit speed. Legato is much easier for speed, but playing an even triplet is more difficult.

To be sure of even finger control throughout the exercise we will apply the 'rotation' approach that was taught in example 3.

Study the following:

Example 16a:

Pick through this example slowly using fingers 4, 2 and 1. Set the metronome to 70 and begin by playing three notes per beat (half the written speed of the above example). Try to accent each note occurring on the 12th fret.

When you can complete example 16a accurately, try playing the loop twice around before stopping. Increase this to three repeats, and finally loop the whole example as in **example 16b:**

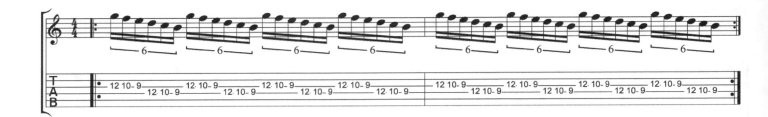

Begin to speed up example 16b by setting your metronome to 35bpm and playing the example as the notated 1/16th-note triplets, i.e. six notes per click. As you get comfortable, increase the metronome by increments of 4bpm.

Soon, most people find that their technique and rhythm starts to break down. When this happens, go back to example 16a and play through the first six notes, pausing while the click continues to beat one. In other words, play all six notes of the cycle, and pause when you land on the first note again. Don't worry yet about evenly spacing your notes, just try to cram in all six notes and land on the first again.

The trick we use now is to add in an obstacle, in this case a string-skip:

Example 16c:

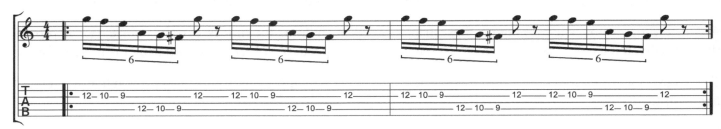

Either keep the tempo the same, or slightly increase it by 8bpm, and try to get around the loop. Forget about rhythm, but just try to complete the cycle to land on the first note again. You picking should remain the same.

Then try two loops before pausing.

Finally, reduce your metronome speed to the tempo where you originally got stuck and play this:

Example 16d:

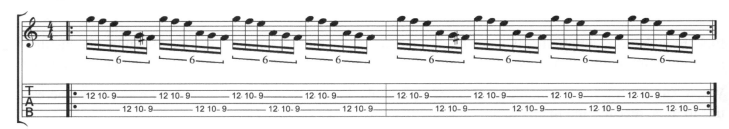

Don't worry too much about even note spacing, just concentrate on getting back to the first note on the click.

This will feel weak and out of time, however, when you go back to playing the original loop (example 16a) at the speed where you initially got stuck, you will find it much easier to play. Now you can again focus on rhythm and accuracy.

Explore every rotation of the exercise and look for weaknesses to work on.

Example 16e:

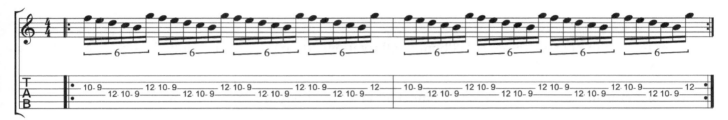

Example 16f:

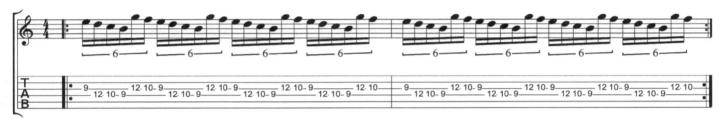

Example 16g:

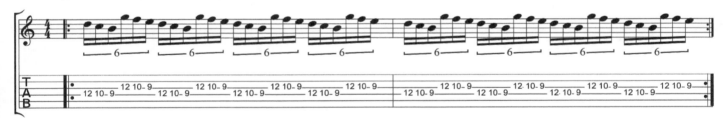

Example 16h:

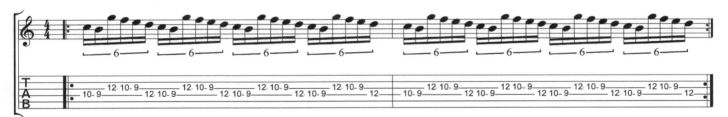

Example 16i:

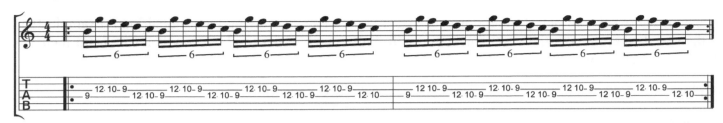

The target for 1/16th note exercises is 100bpm in all rotations. If you get stuck, apply the obstacle method to help you increase your speed.

The other patterns in which you should be competent in all rotations are shown below:

Example 17a:

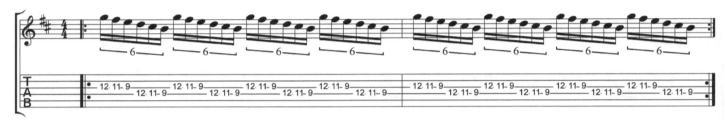

Example 17b:

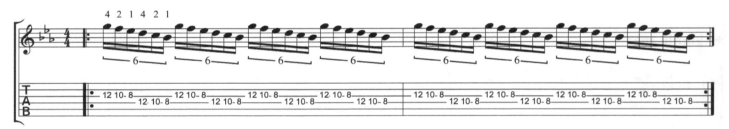

Example 17c:

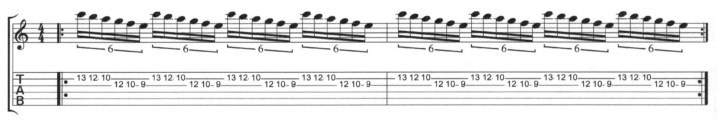

Example 17d:

Practice these in the same way as before and use the obstacle trick when you hit a brick wall.

Remember, if you feel any pain, take a break and see a doctor. The most likely reason is that you're trying to play too fast, too soon. Always warm up!

Rhythm

"The Right Note Played at the Wrong Time is Still a Wrong Note."

This chapter works on your fundamental sense of time. Your internal clock is probably the most important factor in how well you play your instrument. The great news is that the examples in this section have the most immediate and far reaching benefits in your playing.

One of the inherent rhythmical problems with the guitar is that it is easy to play quickly and slur notes together. Unlike other instruments, you don't have to take a breath in order to play a note so there is nothing physical that forces you to stop playing note. To make a lot of notes sound quickly, legato is a relatively simple technique.

Fast notes 'squashing' together between the beat is something we will examine in great detail later, however before we tackle that, we will work on your sense of where the beat actually *is!*

Imagine an American football[4] pitch; the white lines are there to help us divide up the space and judge what yardage was gained before the player gets knocked down. The white lines on the football pitch, for as us musicians, are like all the Hi-Hats, Snares, Kicks and Toms in a drum groove. If we were to remove all the white lines from the football pitch, we would have to work very hard on our perception of distance to judge exactly where the man fell. In this section, we will learn to hear and feel these distances without the while lines.

We will strip back the drum kit, removing all the excess notes until just beats two and beat four, (the snares), remain.

Hearing the Metronome on Beats Two and Four

The following section may be challenging at first, but stick with it because developing these skills is the most important thing you can do for your playing.

Set your metronome to 35bpm[5].

Say out loud 'two', and then 'four' on each successive click. This is a basic *back beat* on a snare drum. When that sits comfortably, fill in the spaces evenly by saying 'one' and 'three' in the spaces. This is tricky, but you'll end up with this:

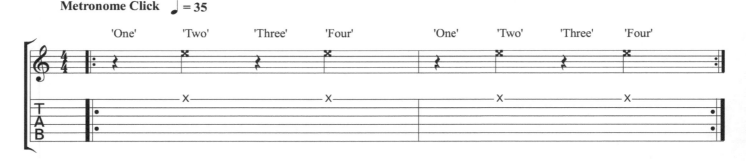

---

4. Or "hand-egg" as we call it in England
5. Some metronomes don't go that slowly. If yours doesn't, it's easy these days to download a free metronome to your smart phone or PC.

Be clear and confident when you count out loud. Confidence here will really help you internalise the beat.

Even Note Groupings

While you count out loud with the click on two and four, play a muted down stroke on a single note or full strum while muting every string.

Example 18a:

Listen extremely carefully to your playing in relation to the click, and notice whether you're slightly ahead of, or behind the beat. Stay with this example until you become relaxed at playing notes on beats one, two, three and four, as the metronome clicks on two and four.

The next stage is to subdivide the 1/4 notes into 1/8th notes. Make sure you keep a steady *down up down up...* with the picking as it will help to keep you in time.

This sounds like the following.

Example 18b:

Again, listen to make sure that the metronome click syncs with every *third* down pick.

Double up once again to start playing 1/16th notes. Don't just listen to the click on two and four though, focus on whether the 1/16th notes are spread evenly across the beat and synchronising with the click.

Example 18c:

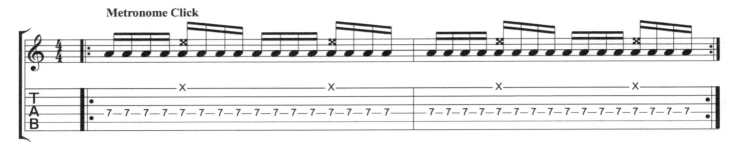

The previous examples will take some time to get together. They are hard but they are also so fundamental to developing good time so spend as long as you can internalising them. When I've taken a break from guitar playing, these are the first exercises I return to.

Triplets

The next example involves playing triplets. It is more difficult, but intrinsic to the important examples that follow.

Before you play, listen to the accompanying audio. Hear to how the triplets are articulated with the plectrum. There is a clear accent on the first of every set of triplets. It is alternate picked and phrased in groups of three.

Accent your picking: DOWN up down Up down up.

Example 18d:

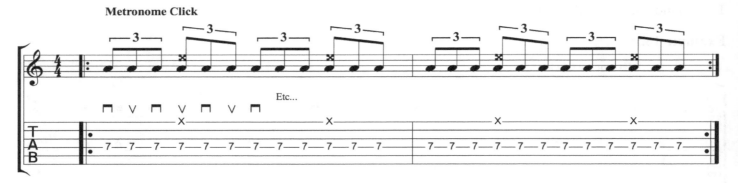

As I mentioned, this example is harder, but it forms a basis for many of the following examples. It takes patience to get it right but you should start to notice an immediate improvement in your rhythmic awareness and note placement.

Switching Between Even Note Groupings

Once the previous examples are taking shape, you should move on to switching between different rhythmic groupings. This is where the real challenges begin.

Study example 18e.

To develop more rhythmic control, we are swapping between 1/4 notes and 1/8th notes. As always, be sure to lock in with the click.

Example 18e:

As you develop more precision, try reducing the metronome speed towards 30. A decrease of 1bpm on your metronome has the effect of a 2bpm reduction in tempo.

Example 18f is the same idea, but we're now moving from 1/8ths to 1/16ths:

Example 18f:

Switching from Even to Odd Note Groupings

I believe that the following is one of the *most important examples in this whole book.*

In example 18g you will learn to change between 1/8th notes and 1/8th note triplets while the metronome clicks a slow two and four.

Example 18g:

Listen carefully to the audio example before you begin. This example is extremely useful is because it counters our natural tendency to *rush into triplets* and fall *slightly behind when moving to straight 1/8ths.*

Play through example 18g and tap your foot on every beat.

While you get to grips with the rhythm, try counting, ¦**1 & 2 & 3 & 4 &** ¦**1 & a 2 & a 3 & a 4 & a** ¦. Keep looping the example until you feel it coming together.

When you think you're getting there, try recording yourself playing against the metronome. This is of huge benefit and a facility that we're lucky to have so easily these days. Be analytical and extremely critical. You will probably notice that when you change into triplets you are playing a bit too quickly and as you move back to 1/8ths you're a little late.

Working to achieve this level of rhythmic precision has a massive effect on our internal sense of time. We're dividing a large time span in our head, (the slow two and four click) while also having to control a physical and mental shift between playing even and odd groupings. It truly is steroids for your brain's rhythmic 'muscle'.

If you do not currently have a guitar teacher, practise with a friend. Record yourself as often as you can and be honest and objective about your accuracy. Hard work here will pay many dividends in the future. Try not to get frustrated if these exercises take a while to master, they're not easy.

Another common rhythm change is moving from triplets to straight 1/16th notes. In the following example, you will encounter many of the same problems as in example 18g, but if you've put the time into studying example 18f it won't be too bad.

Example 18h:

Remember to slow the tempo down when the examples starts to feel easier.

Next, focus on moving between straight 1/16th notes and 1/16th-note triplets. This can be a challenge because of the speed. Don't forget that a bpm of 35 on your metronome generates a tempo of 70. Find a speed which is a good compromise between technique and rhythmic control.

Example 18i:

Extended Rhythmic Combinations

The following examples will be a tough test of your rhythmic control. Always record your playing and listen back to is analytically.

Example 18j:

Example 18k:

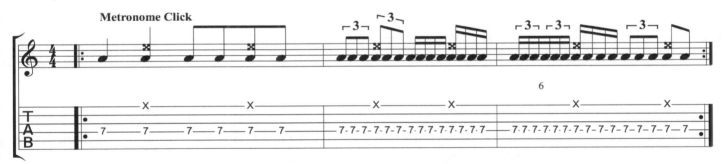

Melodic Rhythm

While it's great to practice these example on one note to develop solid time, we obviously have to be able to apply these rhythms in a melodic context. You already know that different fretting-hand finger combinations have different weaknesses, so it's vital to know we can control rhythm when playing 'normally'. To practice straight 1/8th notes, we will use an A Major Scale.

Example 19a:

With the metronome at 30bpm and clicking on beats two and four, play examples 18a to 18f. Apply this process to all of the examples from the Picking Chapter of this book. The scale examples in particular will work well.

Practice switching between even 1/8ths and triplets.

Example 19b:

Practicing in this way contextualises the rhythms that you have been studying into real, useful melodic forms and so helps to internalise the information.

Riff - Solo - Riff

One of the best ways to practice 'locking down' the time of a piece is to play a simple riff with a two and four metronome backbeat, and switch between playing one bar of a riff and one bar of an improvised solo.

Most people *think* they can play a bit of a blues. The following ideas really let you see how tight your time is. When this example was first given to me, I was shocked at just how much work I needed to do. I work on similar ideas every day in practice and still find them beneficial.

The key to this is starting *extremely* simply with your solo.

I have notated a simple blues idea in example 20a. It revolves around a repeating triplet blues riff that you should first make sure you can play in time. Before attempting the triplet solo fills, your rhythm playing should be perfect. Every time you use your 3rd finger to play the 4th fret, the metronome should be *perfectly* synced with the movement.

Example 20a:

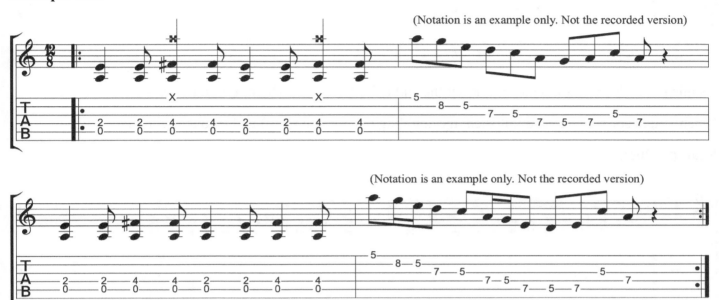

As you start to *lock in* to the time and feel, start adding improvised blues lines every second bar. A couple of minor pentatonic ideas are shown in the previous example. It is not necessary to learn these lines, and they are not played as written on the accompanying audio file; just improvise for a few beats in triplets and concentrate on coming back to the blues riff precisely in time.

It is always interesting to see how difficult most people find this. I suddenly see students who *were* whizzing around the fretboard, start struggling to nail even the simplest of minor pentatonic blues licks. Don't be frustrated if this happens to you, see at as an opportunity to consolidate your technique and rebuild from stronger rhythmic foundations. It doesn't take *that* long to build up to the level you were playing at before, but when you get there everything you play will be that much more in time and effective.

Here is a variation of example 20a, but this time the riff is a straight-ahead rock guitar groove. It will help you practice even 1/8ths, 1/16ths and 1/16th-note triplets.

Example 20b:

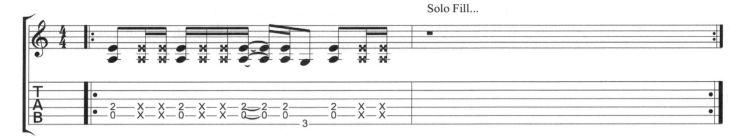

As this is a little more intricate, check out the audio file to hear the rhythm if you need to.

When you become more accomplished, try doubling the amount of riff and solo that you play.

Example 20c:

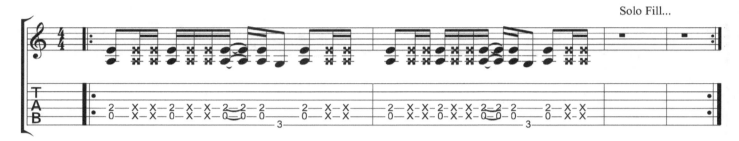

Nuno Bettencourt from *Extreme* is a master of this kind of riff/fill idea.

A useful way to test your rhythmic control is to play a continuous scale loop against a metronome clicking on beats one, two, three and four and programming it to be silent every other bar. Not many metronomes do this, but if you have access to a sequencer like Pro Tools, Sibelius, Cubase or Garage Band, these things are easy to program. Start with the tempo at 60bpm, and then try ascending and descending the following scale idea.

Example 20d:

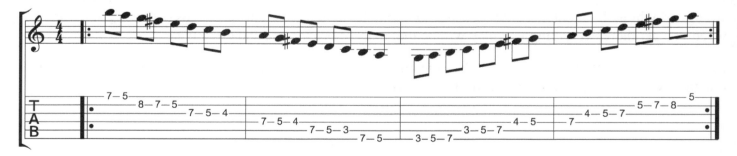

The idea is to make sure that your playing syncs perfectly with the click when it recommences after the bar of silence. If you're feeling brave you can do the same example with the metronome programmed to sound on beats two and four before having a full bar of silence. Keeping the rhythm going for four beats with no click at all is an excellent text of your rhythmic skill. Try this idea with triplets, 1/16th notes, 1/16th-note triplets or any combination of rhythms that you can think of.

1/16th Note Rhythmic Combinations

The rhythms in this chapter are essential vocabulary for all guitarists. They form the foundation of thousands of rock, pop and funk riffs, and you should be able to execute them perfectly. They really are essential to your technical development. To learn them, study the following examples. In particular, pay careful attention to the picking pattern:

Example 21a:

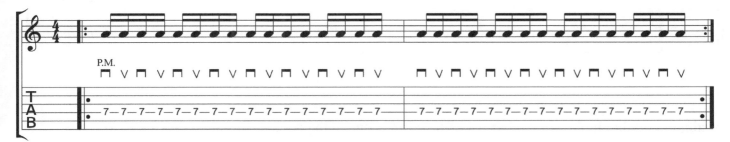

Obviously, this is a simple case of alternate picking throughout. However, I draw your attention to it because it is the basis of the following important concepts. Let's see what happens when vary this rhythm by *missing out* some of the picks in each four-note grouping.

Study the following:

Example 21b:

In example 21b, I tied together the first two notes of each four in the first bar. In musical terms this means play the first note, and hold it for the value of the second.

In other words, pick the first note, hold it for the value of the second and the next pick is on the third note.

Tying two 1/16th notes together in this way creates a single 1/8th note.

The second bar shows *exactly* the same rhythm as the first, it's just written in an easier way to understand.

Look at the picking directions along the bottom line. As we have removed the second note from the rhythm, we simply remove the second pick, (the up-pick) from the sequence.

Executing the rhythm in this way gives us an extremely consistent method by which to control our timing. Listen to the accompanying audio example to hear this played.

In a similar way to the previous example, example 21c ties together the second and third notes of each four-note grouping:

Example 21c:

Again, the rhythm in the second bar is identical to the one in the first.

Play this by missing out the third pick, (a down) in each group of four. Play along with the audio example until you have this internalised.

The final combination is shown below.

Example 21d:

Now we omit the final pick of each beat. The picking is *Down up down. Down up down...*

Let's see what happens when we some of these new rhythmic possibilities.

Example 22a:

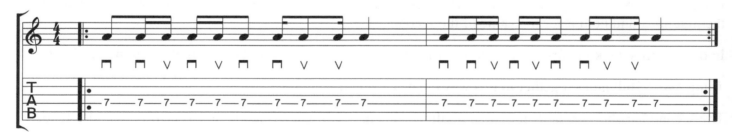

I've added a 1/4 note on beat four to give your picking hand a little bit of a rest between each repeat.

To play the previous rhythm, break each beat down into its individual picking pattern:

Down. Down Up

Down up. Down

Down up. Up

Down

Say the above picking rhythms out-loud and in time with a click at 60bpm to internalise each one before you play it. Listen to the audio example to help you.

Try that rhythm with some muted power chords to create some instant Metallica-style riffs!

Example 22b:

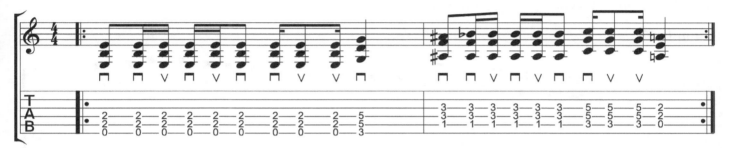

Here are some more picking patterns to get you started, they all work great as funk, rock or fusion rhythm patterns.

Example 22c:

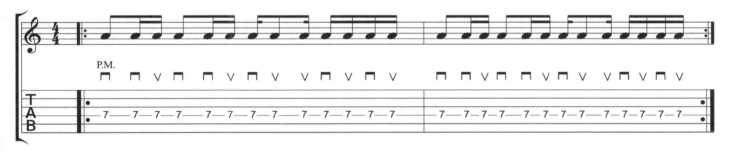

Example 22d:

Example 22e:

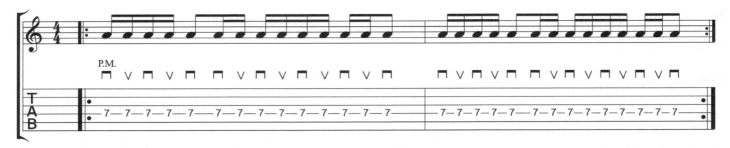

As with example 22b, try making riffs or solos out of each line. You could, for example, try running scales, intervals, triads or arpeggios with the rhythms in this section. Here's an example that uses the rhythm from example 22a on an ascending A Major scale.

Example 22f:

If you practice the above exercise with economy picking you immediately break the 'down up down up' rule of this chapter when you change string. By economy picking, you work on your internal clock and stop relying on picking pattern to execute the line properly.

Legato

Legato means 'in a smooth and flowing manner'. In music, this means the slurring of one note into the next without a discernible gap, or attack between successive notes.

Legato on the guitar is generally handled in one of three ways;

Left hand *hammer-ons*

Left hand *pull-offs*

Right Hand *tapping*

This section examines *hammer-ons, pull-offs* and the unique rhythmic challenges they present us with, due the natural physiology of our hands.

Legato is an essential technique on the guitar as it not only reduces the percussive 'click' of the plectrum on the strings, it also allows us to play extremely quickly by cutting out one of the main obstacles to speed; picking. The challenge though, is to play rhythmic groupings accurately. Rhythmic accuracy is more difficult when playing legato for two main reasons:

We can no longer rely on the plectrum to 'keep time' for us.

Sequential notes on the same string tend to rush into each other, while picking across string changes can fall behind the beat.

The reason that notes on the same string rush into each other is largely down to the physiology of our hands. When you drum your fingers on a table top, there is no natural tendency for them to fall into perfect 1/8th or 1/16th notes, (for example). That 'running together' of your fingers is what we must control as we begin to work on a solid legato style.

Basic Examples

Let's begin by examining the hammer-on.

Notation:

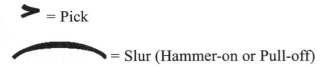 = Pick

= Slur (Hammer-on or Pull-off)

Example 23a:

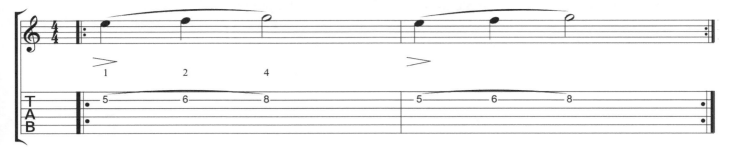

Begin with your 1st finger playing the 5th fret on the B string. Pick it hard and then hammer your 2nd finger down onto the 6th fret. Make sure the 1st finger stays down. Now hammer your 4th finger onto the 8th fret while keeping your 2nd finger down on the 6th.

Listen to the audio example to hear how clean this should sound. When practicing the ideas in this chapter, do not use any distortion on your amp because it will compress the sound and hide any mistakes or weaknesses.

We can reverse the previous idea to work on pull-offs:

Example 23b:

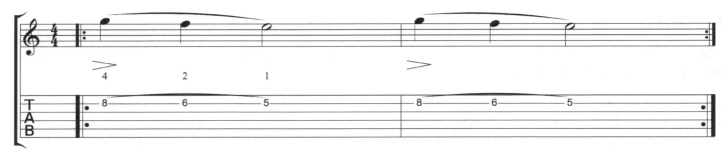

This time, start with *all three* fingers on the B string. Pick the first note and then roll/flick your fingers downwards off the strings to make each successive note sound. Emphasise volume and strength. If you accidently make the adjacent string ring with your pull-off don't worry for now, it'll clean itself up as you develop more control.

Let's combine the two previous examples:

Example 23c:

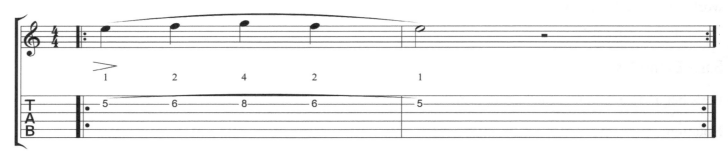

Again, pick only the first note and concentrate on volume and power. Ensure your fingers are bent and that you play on the tips. Any noise coming from the adjacent 1st string should be muted by the pad of your 1st finger.

When you can play the previous example through eight times, try looping it.

Example 23d:

Only pick the first note once, however many repeats you manage. Try to keep the momentum going with the strength in your left hand.

Fret spacings decrease as you ascend the neck so you may find your hand position changing. Also, try the same example played as triplets or 1/16th notes:

Example 23e is an excellent one to develop fretting hand control.

Example 23e:

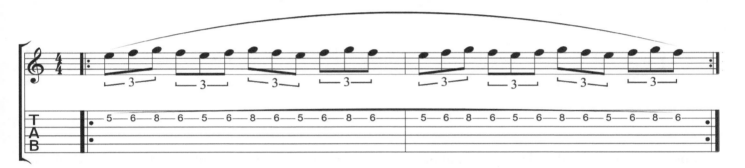

For now, your target should be to play example 23e at 60bpm. If you can go faster, that's great, but listen to the gaps *between* the notes to make sure they're not rushed or falling behind the beat.

Try slowing the above example down to 35 bpm. You will really have to control your fingers to keep the notes even.

Legato With All Four Fingers

The next example develops control of all four fingers of the fretting hand. As always, only pick the first note of each group.

Example 24a:

Try the previous example at 50 bpm. Make sure every hammer-on is accentuated on the beat.

Once again move this example onto different strings and frets. Try the example on frets 1-4 and you will notice a big increase in the difficulty.

Now go back and attempt some of the earlier finger permutation examples in the first chapter, but now only pick the first note on each string. Here's one example.

Example 24b:

Most of the exercsies in the picking section of this book can be re-written as legato workouts, so be creative with your practice.

This finger strength example you saw in section one is great to revisit as a legato exercise.

Only pick the first note on each string. Aim to play this example at 80bpm and if you encounter any pain or discomfort, stop playing immediately and consult a specialist.

Example 24c:

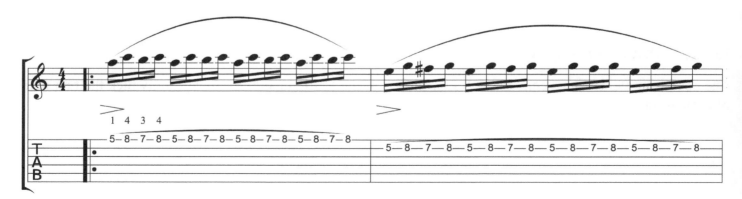

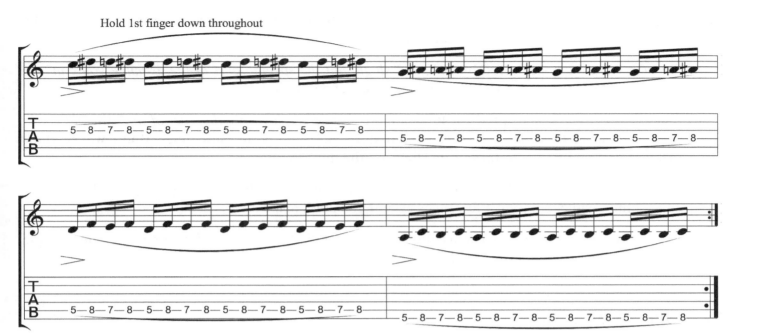

Speeding up the Fretting Hand

The trick to developing legato speed is to do it in little bursts. Instead of going 'all out' to play as fast as possible for as long as possible, bring speed into your playing in short sections. This example, with the tempo set to 100bpm, should sort out the majority of technique 'brick walls'

Example 25a:

To keep your rhythm even, focus on locking every note on the 7th fret into the click.

Keep speeding this example up by 8bpm increments. Speeding up in the following way:

1) Set the metronome to, (in this case) 100 bpm and record yourself playing through the example four times.

2) Listen to or watch your recording. If the notes are evenly spaced across the beat, increase the metronome by 8bpm. It is important that you're honest with yourself here.

3) If you get to 140 bpm, halve the metronome speed to 70, and double up the speed of your notes so you are now playing 1/16th notes:

4) Repeat the steps one and two until you find a point at which you're either struggling to play the example, or the rhythm starts to break down.

5) Reduce the metronome speed by 20% and *single out the specific part of the example you can't do.* Whatever it happens to be, isolate it and practice that part only.

6) Increase the metronome speed by 40bpm and continue to play *only the part of the example you're struggling with.* This should be nearly impossible, but try to do it a few times. **Don't worry about perfect timing, just try to target the clicks on the metronome.**

7) Now try completing the full cycle of notes in the above example at the higher speed. This will be almost impossible, but try it a few times even if you don't make it.

8) Finally, set the metronome to 5 bpm **below** where you initially got stuck and continue with the example, increasing the bpm by 8 beats each time.

Speed While Changing Strings

The examples in this chapter develop speed and coordination for string changes on legato runs.

Throughout the examples, pick only the first note on each new string. Also, omit the first pick on each subsequent repeat of the example, as you have already picked the first note on that string at the end of the second bar.

Repeat each example as many times as possible with your metronome set on 80bpm

Example 25b:

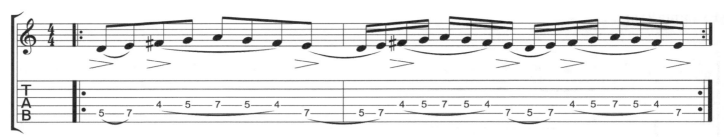

Example 25c:

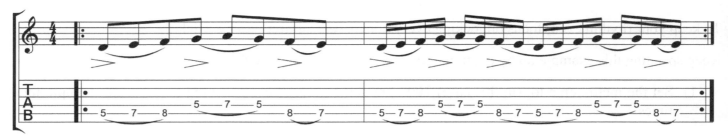

Example 25d:

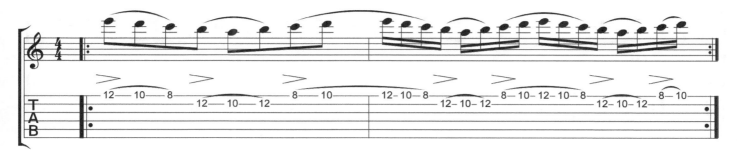

Legato Rotations

In this section, we will revisit the picking examples from examples 7a-7h. However, this time we will use them as legato exercises to ensure our fingers can control the rhythmic divisions perfectly from every point in the rotation. Let's look at what was example 7a:

Example 26a:

As you can see, most of the picks have been removed. We still obey the rules of economy picking, but now we only pick when we change string.

As mentioned previously, the tendency with legato is to *bunch together* notes played consecutively on the same string, and fall slightly behind when changing string. For example, in the above example I would expect students to rush '8, 6, 5,' and '5, 6, 8' and fall behind on a string change.

Set your metronome to 50bpm and play accurately through the above example. Only pick the string changes and *listen carefully to how your notes sync with the metronome*. Playing slowly through this example at first really heightens your awareness of your rhythm in relation to the pulse.

Listening is the most important part of this example. Check out the audio example and listen to how I sync with the click.

To correct the natural physiological tendencies to rush hammer-ons and pull-offs, it is extremely important to look at this example as a rotation, and begin from every note in the sequence as we did in the picking chapter.

The second rotation throws up a challenge.

Example 26b:

This is the same sequence of notes as example 26a. This time, however we begin from the second note of the sequence.

Your 4th finger plays the first note (8) on beat one. When you play it again after the repeat, it is preceded by a '5', on the string above it. This change from beat 'four-and' to beat one is one of the most common weaknesses that I see in students. Learning to control a string change from a higher to a lower string, while landing on the beat with your 4th finger, is an essential lesson in legato timing.

One of the main factors making the example difficult is that you have two picks together, sandwiched by a legato section

Play through the example starting at 50bpm and gradually reduce the metronome speed by 5bpm every time you start to become accurate with your timing. As you slow down you will develop more and more control.

When you can play the example at 30bpm, begin speeding up the metronome in the normal way.

Virtually every rotation of this example throws up a new technical challenge. They all center on controlling your rhythm as you switch between picking and legato during string changes.

The complete series of rotations for this example are as follows:

Example 26a:

Example 26b:

Example 26c:

Example 26d:

Example 26e:

Example 26f:

Example 26g:

Example 26h:

These examples look deceptively simple. They're not! Each one throws up a unique challenge.

In particular, study,

Example 26b: Little finger on the beat.

Example 26d: Three picks together.

Example 26b: Little finger on the beat.

Example 26g: Beat one in the middle of a legato sequence.

Example 26h: Quick changes between 1st and 4th fingers on different strings. Three picks together.

Work slowly, but when you feel assured of your rhythm and time, increase the metronome by 8bpm. Use the speeding-up methods detailed earlier in this book if you get stuck. When you get to 120bpm, set the metronome to 60bpm and continue in 1/16th notes:

Example 26a (played as 1/16th notes):

It might seem odd, but the most powerful tool you have is your foot. *Always* tap your foot to help you place the notes on the beat, especially when you're playing at higher speeds.

Practice this with the other common scale loops from the picking section of this book.

Example 27a:

Example 27b:

The same approach applies to the 1/16th-note triplet rotations you have already studied. Only the first rotation of each example is shown:

Example 28a:

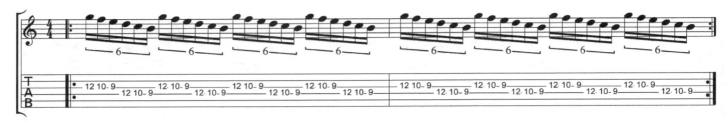

Example 28b:

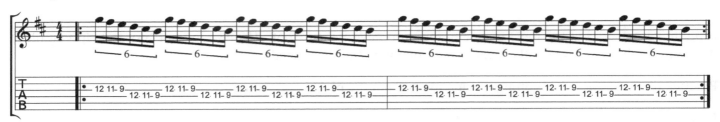

Example 28c:

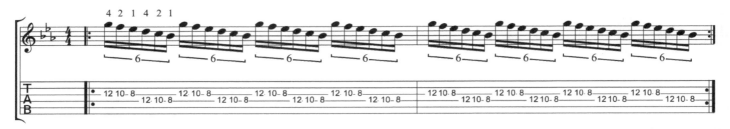

Example 28d:

Example 28e:

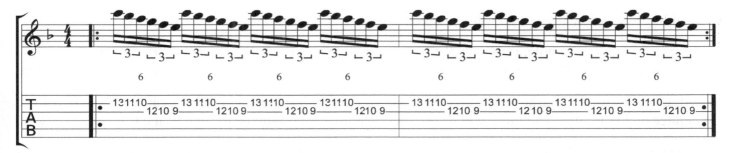

Remember, you can always add in obstacles such as string skips to help you speed up.

Legato With Open Strings

Legato, with pull-offs to open strings, is a common and useful technique. It is employed to great effect by many guitarists. A fantastic example is Joe Satriani's *Summer Song* at around 01:55.

To work on our open-string technique we will study the following idea.

Example 29a:

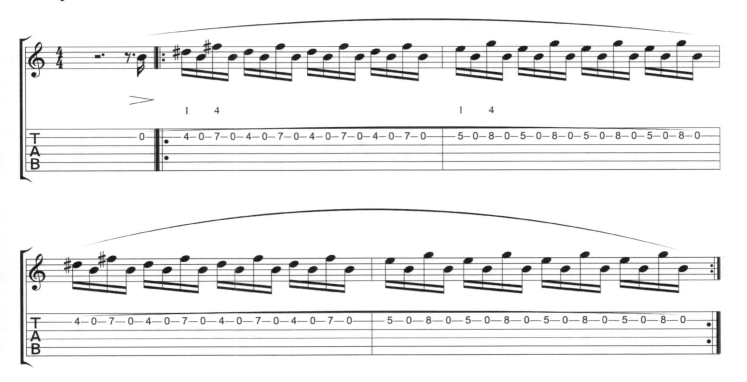

The challenges in the above example lie in two areas:

- Accidently sounding the 1st string when you do a pull-off,

- Building strength with the 1st / 4th finger combination.

As this is as a legato example, pick *only* the first note of the sequence; the open 'B' string. From that point, every single note should be hammered on from 'nothing' by the left hand or pulled off back to the open string.

At first, it is okay to sacrifice accuracy for strength if you have never played in this style before. You may have to hammer-on harder than you think you need. Every hammer-on should be as loud as the first initial pick.

When you pull-off, really give it some energy. You might catch the open 'E' string at first but for now, strength and volume are more important.

Build speed and stamina over a period of a few days. As you continue to develop strength, concentrate on making the movements of your fretting fingers smaller while retaining the volume of each note. Each legato note should be as loud as the first initial pick.

If you keep catching the open 'E' string by accident, try rolling your fretting hands lightly round the neck so that your fingers move towards you. The *side* of your index finger should always be in light contact with the bottom of the neck. If you are doing this correctly, the flesh of the index finger will be in contact with the high 'E' string and keep it muted.

When you're ready, add some distortion and concentrate on keeping each note clean.

The next part of the exercise tests you by jumping around the neck a bit more:

Example 29b:

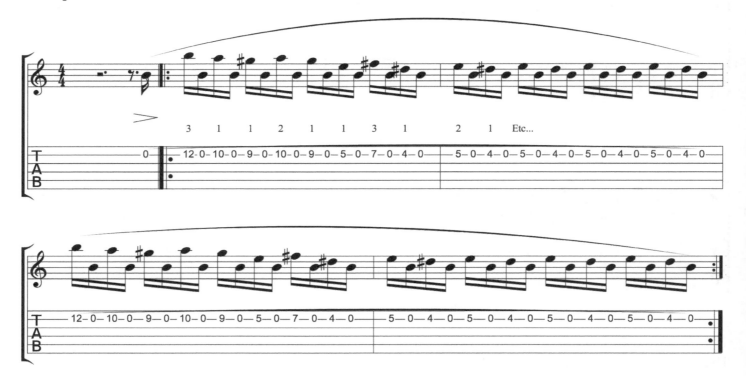

This gives you the opportunity to work on the strength and accuracy of your 1st and 2nd fingers over larger intervals. Approach it in the same way as example 29a.

The following G Minor Blues scale idea is a great exercise for combining open string picks and open string pull-offs. Pay attention to the picking. The picked notes create a polyrhythmic feel by articulating unusually placed notes and sounds excellent when sped up.

Example 29c:

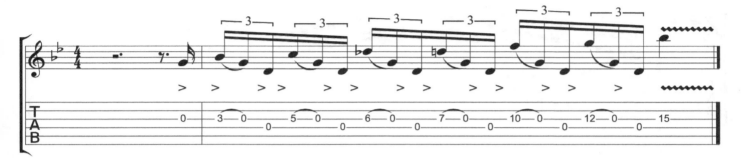

See if you can continue the above idea up the neck into the second octave.

An extension of the above example could involve double pull-offs for an even more unusual effect, ala Joe Satriani:

Example 29d:

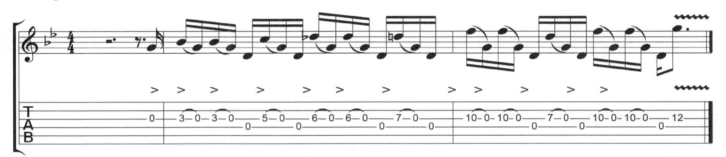

Using Two- and Three-note-per-string Scales

Before we look at the application of the 'classic' three-note-per-string legato runs popularised in the '70s and '80s, I believe it is important to take a look at *modal* scale shapes that use both two-, and three-note-per-string combinations. By learning legato fingerings across scales with different numbers of notes on each string, you will quickly improve the rhythmic control of your fretting hand.

Remember, certain fingering combinations will be stronger than others and the tendency will be to rush the 3 note groups and fall behind the technically more challenging two-note groupings.

Begin by memorising each shape as a separate entity before using the metronome. Start at whatever speed is comfortable, normally about 60bpm if you're playing 1/16th notes and don't worry too much about specific fingerings for scales.

Work on only one scale shape at a time, for example, for the first week you might work on shape 1, the second week, shape 2 etc.

The first stage is to get confident ascending and descending each shape with *good rhythm*. Picking only the first note on each string, you should be able to execute these shapes in 1/16th notes without *any* rhythmic deviation as you change from a two-, to a three-note grouping across the strings. To become secure of this, try playing the shapes in 1/8th notes at 40bpm.

The following scales are written out as modes of G Major.

Example 30a: Shape 1

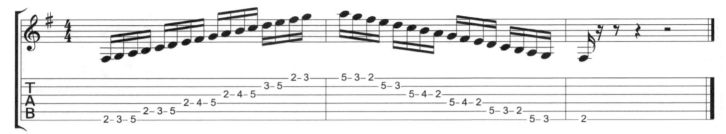

Example 30b: Shape 2

Example 30c: Shape 3

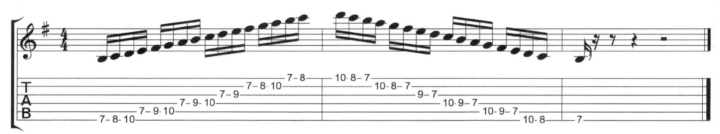

Example 30d: Shape 4

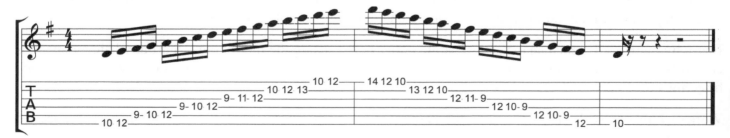

Example 30e: Shape 5

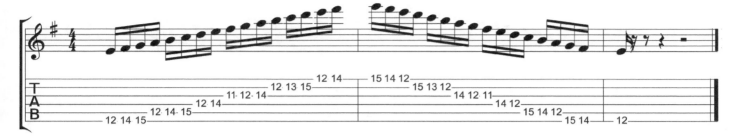

As you begin to develop more control across all six strings, apply some of the 1/16th note rhythmic subdivision ideas from earlier.

Three-Note-Per-String Scales

You may already know that the scales in the previous chapter can be arranged as seven, three-note-per-string scale shapes. These are commonly used for fast, 1/16th-note triplet runs, although you should definitely learn them as straight 1/16ths to develop yet more control in your fretting hand. Here are a few of the more commonly used, three-note-per-string scale shapes.

These patterns should be learned in the same way as in previous sections. Strive for rhythmic perfection and strong, clear notes while you explore interval skips, scales patterns, triads and arpeggios.

The following are for reference only and not included as audio examples:

Example 31a:

Example 31b:

Example 31c:

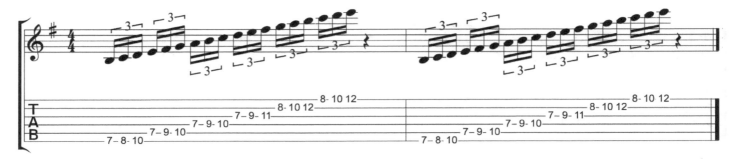

Example 31d:

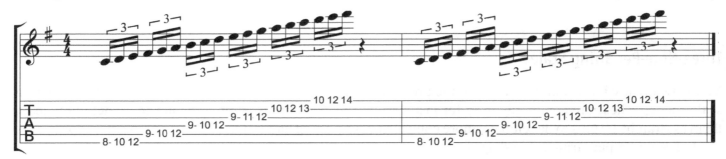

Example 31e:

Example 31f:

Example 31g:

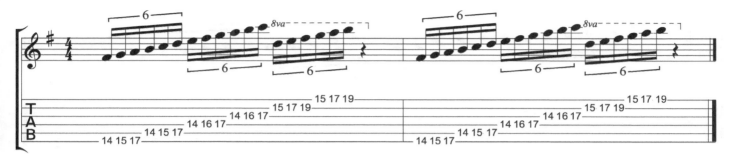

Three-Note-Per-String Patterns and Fragments

If you listen to the majority of 1980's shred guitarists, a large proportion of the fast runs they play are derived from three-note-per-string patterns. Some of the ideas sound a little dated now, but they are an important part of the rock guitar vocabulary. These kinds of patterns are virtually limitless, but the majority rely on consistent, simple, fingering and regular rhythmic phrasing.

While most of the fingering on the fretboard is fairly straightforward, some patterns can be extremely awkward to finger across strings or position shifts. In the past when I have transcribed these ideas, if something is very difficult to play, it is normally because I have been placed it in the wrong position on the neck. If you find an area of the neck where a pattern is particularly difficult, avoid it and play somewhere else!

Here are some legato (or picked) patterns you should know. I have written out the essence of the idea but it will be more beneficial to you to learn to apply each idea in a different area of the neck by yourself.

Example 32a:

Example 32b:

Example 32c:

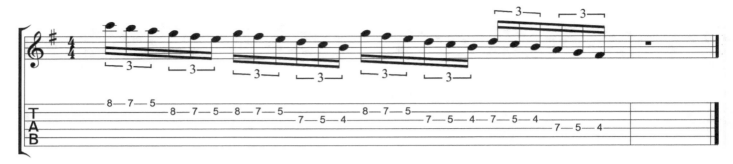

Example 32d:

Example 32e:

Example 32f:

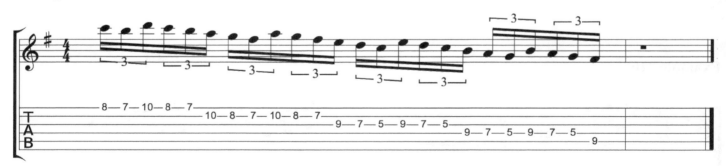

Example 32g:

Example 32h:

Legato on Single Strings

Ascending or descending the neck using legato patterns on single strings is a vital tool that aids melodic continuation of an idea. It is an extremely useful tool for position shifting and helps create those modern lines which seem to ascend forever.

The trick is to give serious consideration to the finger with which we position-shift. In the following examples pay careful attention to the notated fingering. Also, a vital part of the example is to keep the sound ringing as you slide between positions. Keep firm contact between the fingertip and the string and slide as hard as you can.

Example 33a:

Example 33b:

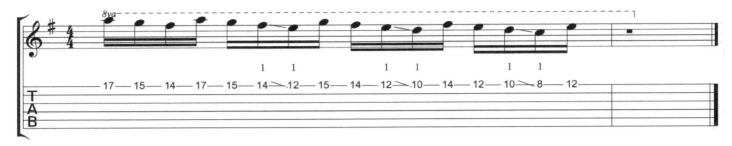

Example 33c:

Example 33d:

Try these examples on every string to make sure you can do them without hitting the ones adjacent. Also, these examples are written out in the key of G. Try them in as many other keys as you can.

Expressive Techniques

This section goes back to the premise that *you are what you practice*. If you only play technical, pattern-based exercises, your music will come across as cold and clinical. Your audience responds more deeply to emotion and feel in music, than displays of sheer technical prowess[6], so conveying the passion and energy you feel is essential.

Of course, this is a difficult thing to teach; I can't just reach down into your soul and pull out your feelings! What I can show you here are the musical techniques that often go hand in hand with more emotive playing.

Remember that the most emotive players, (to my mind at least), are never the ones that play everything perfectly from a technical point of view. They are the ones who throw their heart and soul into the music. The odd technical flaw is more than made up for with a judicious use of dynamics and phrasing.

Once again, *how much technique do you need?* Don't you think you should be spending your time actually making your music connect with your audience?

Vibrato

In my opinion, vibrato is the most important expressive effect. It gives your phrases a vocal quality and makes your music sing. There are many types, but here we will focus on just two, *axial*, and *radial*.

Axial vibrato is when you quickly and repeatedly pull the string slightly sharp, *parallel* to the guitar string.

Radial vibrato is more similar to string bending; your wrist moves in a direction perpendicular to the guitar string, using a finger as a pivot on the underside of neck. This is more difficult, but it does give extremely worthwhile results.

Axial Vibrato

To create axial vibrato, you simply press firmly on a fretted note and, making sure your wrist is soft, move your wrist quickly backwards and forwards parallel to the neck of the guitar. Often, your thumb will quickly release from the back of the neck to help with the speed of the wrist movement. This movement, combined with the pressure you place with your fingertip repeatedly pulls the string slightly sharp before releasing. This is an easy technique that gives life and dynamics to your music whenever there is a longer, sustained note.

Axial vibrato is a subtle effect, and it is important to practice it with each finger of the fretting hand. It is much harder to produce good vibrato with the 4th finger than the 1st.

Here is one exercise to help you develop effective axial vibrato:

---

6. Not that the two things are mutually exclusive.

Example 34a:

Try removing your thumb from the back of the guitar neck to allow your wrist to move more quickly and evenly.

Practice moving between slow to fast and back to slow vibrato for added effect. This is demonstrated in audio example 34a part 2.

Try the above example in different areas of the guitar neck and on different strings. They all feel different and require different types of control.

Add this kind of vibrato to any musical phrases or licks that you know. Take into account the tempo and groove of the song; you might want to sync your vibrato into 1/8th, 1/16th or 1/32 notes.

Radial Vibrato

Radial vibrato is a more difficult technique; it creates *much* wider vibrato which can often be up to a tone wide. Some guitarists go as far as to add vibrato which is a tone and a half wide when playing hard rock and fusion.

With radial vibrato we must greatly alter the position of the hand on the guitar neck so that we can *bend* the desired note up and down quickly. This involves using the *outside* part of the finger on the string, (so that your fingernail points straight down the neck towards you), and using the first finger as a lever or *pivot* against the underside of the neck to aid quick, repeated bends.

If you imagine your wrist turning a door knob, or the Queen of England waving, you will get the idea.

Radial vibrato is an individual technique which tends to be unique to each guitarist, however I will describe the method by which I get the best results. You may want to alter the following steps which apply to vibrato on the *1st* finger as you see fit. The ultimate goal is to achieve the ability to execute *tone wide* vibrato with *each* finger of the fretting hand.

1) Play and hold the desired note. Try playing the 7th fret on the 3rd string, with your 1st finger.

2) Roll your wrist *away* from you, so instead of playing the note with the tip of the 1st finger you are playing on its side. Pushing your elbow out away from you will help with this.

3) The nail of your first finger should now be pointing straight down the string towards you.

4) Push your 1st finger up, into the underside of the neck. It should connect with the neck just below the knuckle closest to your palm.

5) Let your thumb creep over the top of the neck and relax your wrist, so your unused fingers fall and fan out slightly.

6) Using your already-placed 1st finger as a pivot, turn your wrist *away* from you to bend the string down towards the floor, pulling it slightly sharp.

7) Relax the pressure in your wrist and hand to let the string release back to its starting position.

8) Repeat this as many times as you can.

At first you won't move the string far and it may become sore on the side of your finger quite quickly. When this happens take a break.

As you get stronger and your skin becomes tougher, you will be able to move the string further and more quickly. The key to all this, is to always use the *side* of the finger, and always have a pivoting finger under the neck.

I like to build redundancy into my playing, so I spend time practicing bending the string much further than I would ever realistically use. If you can work your way up to a tone-and-a-half vibrato then you're doing well. In my playing, I normally aim for a semi-tone.

The following examples will help you develop vibrato strength, depth and speed on all fingers.

Example 34b: 1st finger.

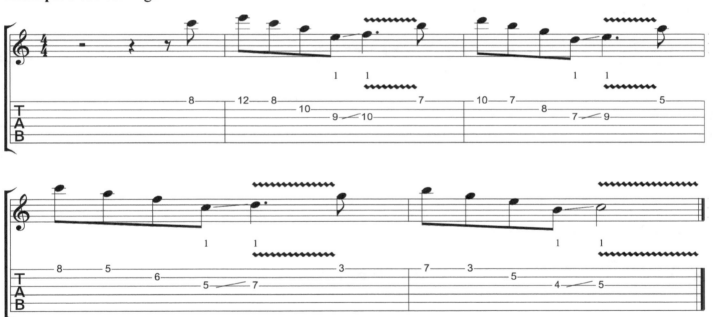

Example 34c: 2nd finger.

Example 34d: 3rd finger.

Example 34e: 4th finger.

It is difficult and unusual to place the 4th finger on its side in the same manner as the other fingers. You should still roll it slightly, but use your other fingers placed on the string behind to add strength and support.

Vibrato is a difficult technique that may take longer to develop than the other skills in this book. Try to spend five minutes every day working on your depth, speed and coordination with each finger. Try the ideas in this section over different string groupings, and in different positions on the guitar. Vibrato is much more difficult towards the lower frets.

Bending

Bending notes with perfect intonation is a skill that really sets the professionals apart from amateurs. Aside from good rhythm, developing perfect intonation is a priority for all my students when they start playing guitar. Nothing ruins a good solo more than an out-of-tune bend.

Once again, it is vital that we learn to bend accurately with each finger, and your 2nd, 3rd and 4th fingers should be capable of executing up to a *one-and-a-half tone* bend.

To bend a note on the guitar you should always support the bending finger with any spare fingers below it. In other words, if you are bending a note on the 3rd string, 7th fret with your 3rd finger, your 2nd finger (if not also your 1st) should also be on the string to add power and control.

The idea behind all the examples in this chapter is to play a reference note, descend the string a few frets and then bend perfectly back up to the reference. Treat this as an aural example; you are listening for the bent note to sound exactly like the reference pitch.

Try the following three examples with different fingers on each bend. Go through each line four times. First, bend with your 1st finger, then your 2nd etc. Don't worry about bending with your 1st finger for the tone-and-a-half bends, it is unnecessary to develop that kind of power right now.

Example 35a: Semitone bends.

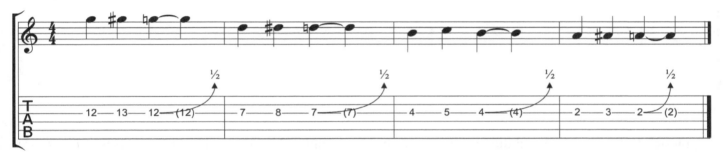

Example 35b: Tone bends.

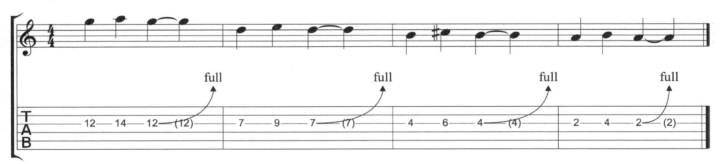

Example 35c: Tone-and-a-half bends.

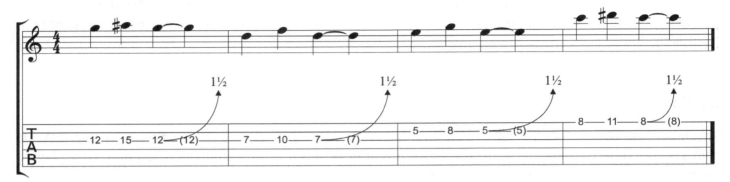

Begin by bending each note very slowly to pitch. this will give you time to hear if you are in tune. It will also develop strength and control in your fingers.

Gradually speed up the rate at which you bend to the target note. If you can hit it perfectly with an immediate, fast bend you know you have it.

Pre-bends

A pre-bend is essentially a bend in reverse. You bend the note to the desired pitch before picking it and releasing the bend. Pre-bends are notated like this:

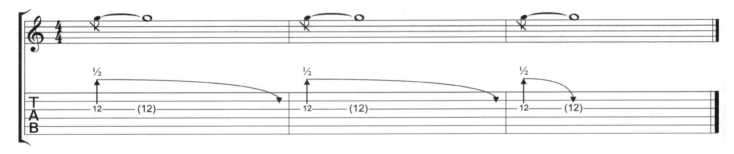

To practice this expressive technique, go back through examples 35a-35c and modify them to include pre-bends in the following way:

Example 35d: Semitone pre-bends.

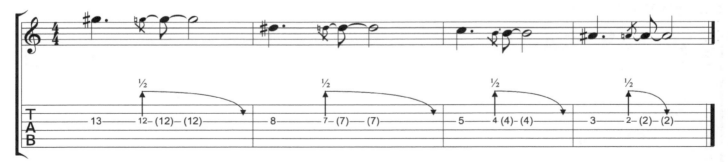

Do this with all fingers and over all bend distances.

Unison Bends

Unison bends are formed when you play two notes together on adjacent strings. The higher note is normally not bent, while the lower note is bent up to sound identical to the higher one. Jimi Hendrix and Jimi Page both made great use of this technique.

These bends are quite difficult to execute on a Floyd Rose tremolo and will always be slightly out of tune due to the nature of the mechanism, but with a bit of vibrato, intonation errors can be covered slightly.

A unison bend is notated in this way:

Example 35e: Unison bends.

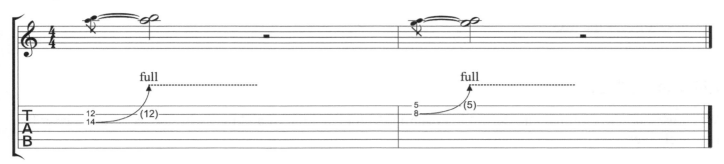

Try the following examples to develop your control and accuracy:

Example 35f: Ascending unison bends

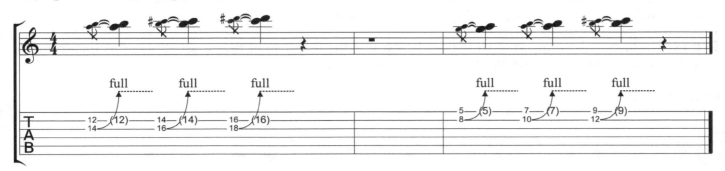

Double-Stop Bends

A double-stop is simply the act of playing two notes at the same time. A double stop bend is when you bend both notes. This is a common technique in blues and rock guitar playing.

To execute a double-stop bend, lay your finger flat, as described in the vibrato section, with your fingernail pointing towards you. However, this time, barre your finger across two adjacent strings. To bend the notes, rotate your wrist in the same manner as vibrato, but only do it once, slowly as you pick both strings. This is shown in the following example:

Example 35g: Double-stop bend

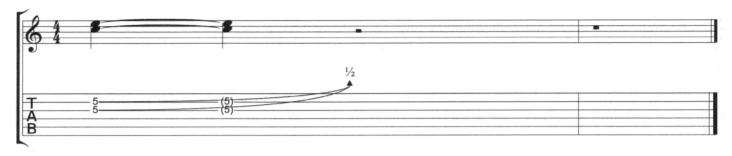

Try these all over the neck.

Filling in the Gaps

When we solo, it is normal and desirable to subtly[7] lead in and out of a phrase with the techniques described in this chapter.

Slowly, and confidently, say the word 'Hey' out loud, speaking from your chest. Notice how the 'H' takes a few milliseconds to form in your chest and throat before the sound comes out of your mouth. Also, if you're sitting in a quiet space, listen carefully to the end of the note. It doesn't end immediately as the sound bounces around the room.

It is those natural phenomena that we seek to recreate with each phrase we play on the guitar. Doing so will give your phrases a musical, vocal quality, setting you apart from most other players.

To flow into lines, it is common to slide from below into the first note of the phrase. Study this line from my book **The CAGED System and 100 Licks for Blues Guitar**.

Example 36a:

The above blues lick in 'A' is written out and played with no decoration. We will be using it as a workhorse to describe the techniques in this chapter, so learn it thoroughly.

---

7. Or not so subtly!

Let's approach the first note with a small slide from below. Put your finger on the *8th* fret on the string, and quickly slide into the first note of the lick. I have repeated this idea on beat four of the second bar, sliding into the 9th fret.

Example 36b:

Experiment by sliding into the first note from further away for a more pronounced effect. For example:

Example 36c:

Often, sliding into a note in this way is simply notated as a slur line into the first note of the phrase.

To mimic the room echo, we can slide off from the notes at the end of each phrase. This is essentially the reverse of sliding in but we need to tail off the note correctly. It's a subtle technique where you gradually reduce the pressure of your finger on the string *during* the slide.

The best way to practice this is to play a single note on the 12th fret, and slide quickly towards the nut. You'll soon figure out how to 'kill' the note before you reach the open string.

The example phrase now sounds like this:

Example 36d:

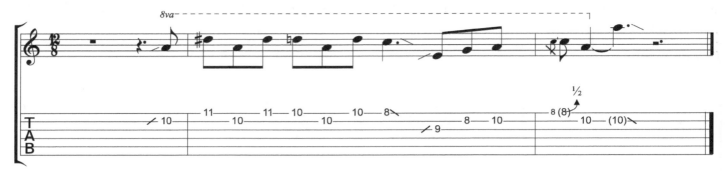

It normally sounds great to add in some wide vibrato before sliding out of a phrase:

Example 36e:

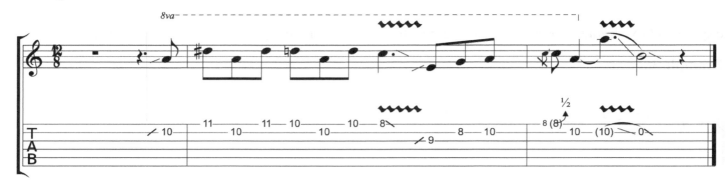

If you have a tremolo arm on your guitar, try sliding out of the phrase all the way to the open string, (don't let the sustain on the note die). As you let the open string sound, slowly depress the bar for an extremely modern approach.

Example 36f:

Compare example 36f with 36a. Listen to how 36f flows as one complete musical phrase.

Grace Notes from Above

Just as we can slide into a note or phrase from below, we can also approach it in the same way from above. This gives an *impassioned, lyrical* quality to any lick. It works well sliding down from the b5 to the 4th of a blues scale, especially when followed by an immediate bend back up to the starting note.

Example 36g:

This idea is used to great effect on For the Love of God from Steve Vai's Passion and Warfare album.

Natural Harmonics

Harmonics on the guitar are the result of a physical effect caused by placing a static *node* on the guitar string, causing it to resonate over two different lengths[8].

There are many ways to generate harmonics on the guitar which all create different effects. The main ways will be detailed here but the topic really deserves a book to itself.

The first mechanism most people come across when playing with harmonics is the *natural* harmonic. This type of harmonic requires the least manipulation of the guitar and occurs naturally at many specific points on each string.

The idea is to create a small point on a string which is absolutely still when you pick the string. This point splits the string into two separate resonating parts.

Starting at the 12th fret on the 3rd string, touch the stringgently *directly above the fret bar* with a fretting hand finger as you pluck the open string with your picking hand. When you pick the string, simultaneously lift off the fretting finger to let the harmonic ring out.

---

8. This is a massive over simplification, but a detailed analysis of the physics of harmonics is well outside the scope of this book.

Example 37a:

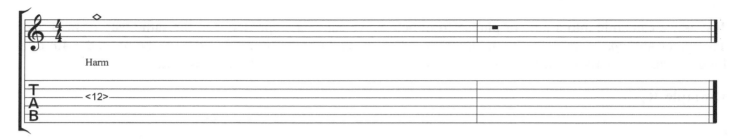

The process can be applied to notes on the 7th and 5th fret, as you descend the fretboard the notes get more difficult to produce:

Example 37b:

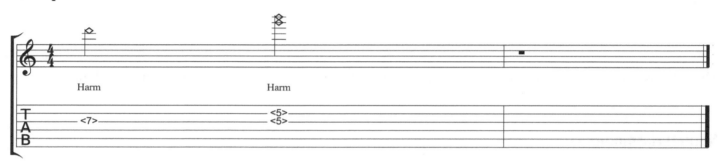

Keep experimenting by moving your finger down towards the nut. There are harmonics at the.4th fret, the 3.9, the 3.2 and the 2.7 in increasing order of difficulty to produce. If you are struggling, try adding a bit of gain or distortion on your amp.

All of the above harmonic locations are doubled identically 12 and 24 frets above. For example, the 5th fret harmonic can also be played at the 17th or at the equivalent of the 29th fret.

Natural harmonics can also be played as double stops:

Example 37c:

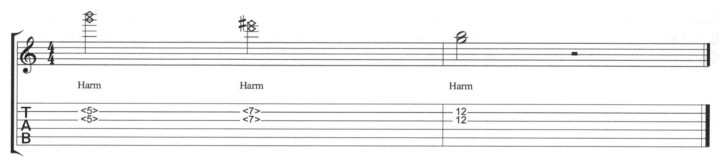

Or they can be played sequentially to make a melody:

Example 37d:

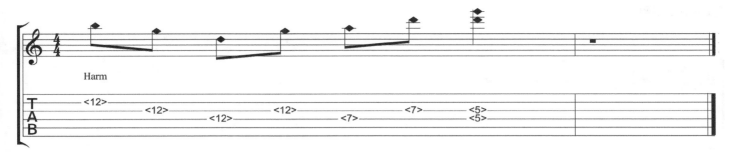

A final trick is to play a double stopped harmonic and then slowly dive-bomb the whammy bar. As the strings are different tensions they will lower in pitch at different rates causing an excellent, out-of-phase, effect which sounds great with distortion:

Example 37e:

Tapped Harmonics

Tapped harmonics have some similarities with natural harmonics, in that they are created in specific intervals above a fundamental tone. However, they are produced by first playing a note with the fretting hand and then reaching over with the *picking* hand and tapping directly on the fret-wire a set distance above the fretted note. The distances you can tap above the fundamental are the same as in the previous chapter.

In the first example, pick the 2nd fret on the 3rd string as normal, and then with the middle finger of your right hand, tap quickly, almost bouncing off the 14th fret on the same string.

Example 38a:

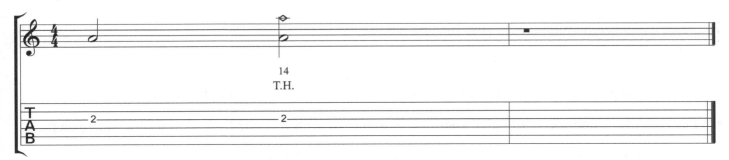

You can produce a harmonic by tapping 12, 9, 7 or 5 frets above the picked note:

Example 38b:

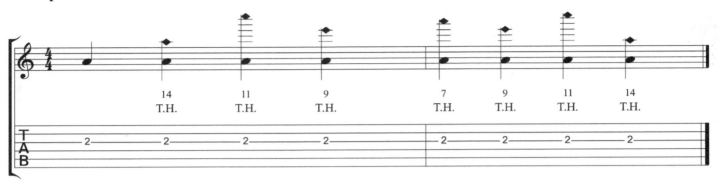

These taps get a bit trickier as you descend the neck, but you can help by giving the fretting note a bit of vibrato.

A great technique is to bend the fretted note *before* tapping the harmonic.

Example 38c:

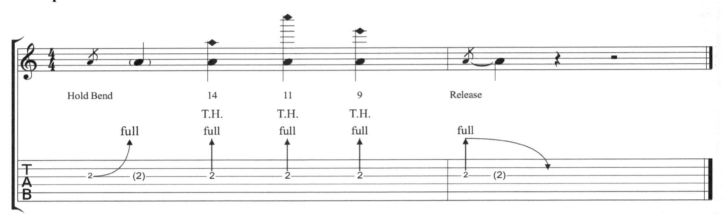

Pinched Harmonics

Pinched harmonics are artificially created by using the thumb of the picking hand to make contact with the string, *immediately* after you pick a note. This movement is so quick you could consider it simultaneous. As always, there are only certain locations on the string where you can make pinched harmonics, and they relate to the previously mentioned 'nodes' on the string. The best way to find these points is to experiment by moving your right-hand picking position slowly towards the neck while applying vibrato to a fretted note. It is easier with some distortion on your amp.

To create a pinched harmonic with your picking hand:

• Pinch your plectrum so that it lies almost at right angles to the string.

• Place the fingernail of your index finger on the desired string, (we will use the 3rd string).

• Push the plectrum firmly through the string and aim to catch it with the flesh of your thumb as you pick.

• Try the above steps while applying vibrato to the 3rd fret on the 3rd string.

- If no harmonic is generated, shift your picking hand 1 or 2mm towards the neck and try again.

If you are really struggling to play the harmonic, make sure you have two points of contact as you pick the string, your thumb and your pick. Sliding down the index finger nail helps a lot too. If you're fretting the 3rd fret and you're playing a strat-oid, guitar there will be a harmonic about halfway between the neck and middle pickups. Lots of vibrato in your fretting hand will help a lot too.

This is a tricky technique to learn, but once you have it, it will stay with you.

It's hard to find two pieces of music which notate pinched harmonics the same way twice, there really is no convention. Normally a music book will have a glossary of common techniques and how they're written, although one common way is this:

Example 38d:

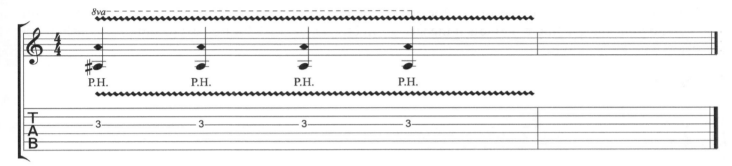

The numbers on the tab stave are often written inside diamonds or triangles.

Listen to example 38e, I play it through twice, the first time it is played as written, the second time I liberally use pinched harmonics for a more modern rock effect:

Example 38e:

As you play through the phrase, experiment with your picking hand position. Move it towards and away from the bridge, try moving it forward *as you play the line* so that you hit pinched harmonics in different spots during the phrase. This is a lot of fun to experiment with and produces some great results!

The famous 'Satch Scream' is produced by depressing the whammy bar, playing double-stop pinched harmonics on the open 2nd and 3rd strings and slowly bringing up the bar.

Harp Harmonics

Harp, or *artificial,* harmonics are an extremely beautiful sound. They are created by touching the string with a finger of the *picking hand* just as you pick the string. They are created on the same nodes as described previously.

To play a harp harmonic, fret a note normally, and reach over onto the neck with your picking hand, 12 frets above the fretted note. Holding the pick normally between your thumb and index finger, gently touch the string 12 frets above the fretted note with your middle finger, (just like with a natural harmonic) and pick the string at the same time with the plectrum.

It's a little awkward at first, but when you remove your picking hand finger, the note should ring out an octave above the fundamental.

In the example below, fret the 2nd fret on the 3rd string, and bring your plectrum all the way up to the 14th fret. Extend your middle finger and touch the string directly above the 14th fret as you simultaneously pluck the string with the plectrum.

Example 38f:

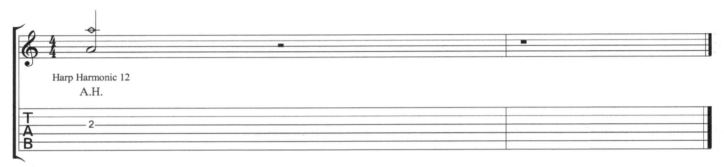

Harp harmonics sound great when you combine them with chords. In the following example, hold down a G Major barre chord and play a harp harmonic, 12 frets above each note:

Example 38g:

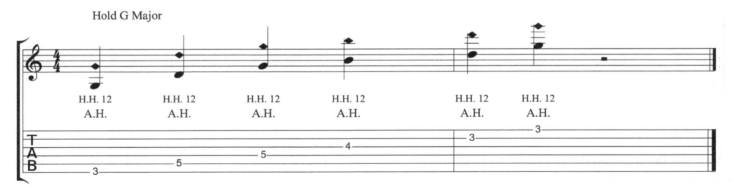

Picking Angle, Position and Dynamics

If you got to see a professional orchestra, it is possible that the lead violinist is playing a £1,200,000 Stradivarius. The bow; just the stick and horse hair they are using can cost upwards of £60,000.

As guitarists, we use a $0.50 piece of plastic.

Virtually every single tone you create on the guitar starts with the pick, so it follows that we have a lot of work to do to get as much good tone out of our plectrum as possible.

There are many factors which we can play with: First of all, changing the angle with which you attack the string creates a *massive* alteration in tone. Try playing a blues lick while holding your pick almost-right-angles to the string,

In the following example, I play the same blues lick three times, the first with a 'normal' pick angle. Next, I angle it at about 80 – 90 degrees throughout, and on the third time I vary the picking angle throughout the phrase.

Example 39a:

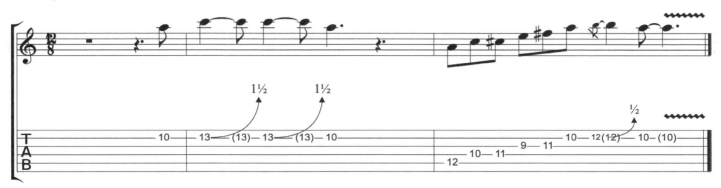

With fairly new strings and a cranked up amp, you will notice a huge difference in your tone and articulaton which your audience will really respond to.

Try varying the location of a picked note. Picking closer to the bridge generates a more 'toppy' sound and gradually working towards the neck will make your tone warmer and fuller.

Combing a change in pick angle with a constantly varying pick position, can give phenomenal results. It's an extremely quick fix to add depth and dynamics to your playing.

My final piece of advice is to practice picking harder than you think you need to. It will help you project the tone through any distortion or effects on your amp.

It's not a one-size-fits-all solution for everything, as picking quietly can be an important effect, but in my experience, most students don't play nearly hard enough. They rely on excess distortion to shape their tone. If you pick harder, you send more signal to the amp. This means that you can use less distortion to get the same effect, and your tone will be instantly improved.

Have Fun!

Made in United States
Troutdale, OR
11/04/2023

14292523R00051